May you flourish
in the Fifth Era.

Best

Matt   Arian

PRAISE FOR
BUILD YOUR FORTUNE IN THE FIFTH ERA

"As someone who has worked with dozens of start-ups and some of the biggest names in Silicon Valley, people ask me all the time how they can be part of today's explosive wealth generation opportunity with the tech economy. This book, with its 10 simple strategies based on an individual's personal goals and resources, provides an excellent roadmap on how anyone can build wealth by investing in the new disruptive innovations that are changing our world."

Susan Butenhoff, CEO Access Emanate Communications

"The authors of the book are exactly the type of people they described so well: 'Angel investors without whom...the whole innovation machine never gets started.' Matthew and Alison actually do what they say and make the Fifth Era benefit us all via educating and supporting entrepreneurs and outlining smart ways to make money during these tectonic transitions. A must read for innovators and investors!"

Alex Fedosseev, CEO 1World Online

"Throughout history, innovation led to prosperity for humankind. Each era changed the rules of the game. The balance of prosperity shifted to those who adapted. Build Your Fortune in the Fifth Era examines lessons learned throughout human evolution. The goal of the book is to decode the rules for the Fifth Era. It maps the game for those seeking wealth in the age of now. This book is a field guide for entrepreneurs, investors, employees and service providers."

Marko Gargenta, Founder PlusPlus and Former Director Twitter University

"The authors have artfully condensed 30 years of innovation-driven experience into a highly engaging book that makes the new "Fifth Era" of disruptive— and highly profitable—innovation accessible to investors, entrepreneurs, and essentially all economic stakeholders. Their work makes a compelling case for why the most valuable companies in the future will be those that align with the new era of technology- and biotechnology- enabled innovations, and how entrepreneurs and investors can harness the profound growth opportunities that are certain to emerge."

Blake Grossman, former CEO, Barclays Global Investors

"Whether you are or just aspire to be an entrepreneur or investor, this book is an invaluable insight into the future. The authors have succinctly captured their decades of experience to help you seize the global opportunities that the Fifth Era presents. A must read."

Priya Guha, Ecosystem General Manager RocketSpace UK

"The authors have been focused on innovation for most of their working careers. This book shares the lessons they have learned as investors, advisors and board directors."

Tony Hsieh, NY Times bestselling author of
"Delivering Happiness," CEO Zappos.com

"*Build Your Fortune in the Fifth Era* is a practical and informative toolkit straight from the heart of Silicon Valley… a must read for anyone looking to make it in today's world!"

Linda Jenkinson, Co-Founder John Paul Group,
Director Air New Zealand/Massey Foundation

"As a veteran Silicon Valley professional who has witnessed the beginnings of this Fifth Era first hand, I can say that the authors' analysis and recommendations ring true. Every young person entering today's workforce would benefit from reading this book, as would anyone else who is open to assessing whether they are truly putting themselves in the best position to take advantage of the extraordinary times we live in. This could be the most impactful book you read this year!"

Riaz Karamali, Partner Pillsbury Winthrop Shaw Pittman LLP

"To read *Build Your Fortune in the Fifth Era* is to gain an appreciation for this unique moment in time when companies leveraging new technologies including cloud, mobile, machine learning, and AI are poised to disrupt every industry. In this easy-to-read guide, Matthew and Alison help their readers understand how best to leverage their individual strengths to capitalize on the great wealth creation to come from the winning disrupters. Kudos to Matthew & Alison for helping make angel investing strategies easy to understand and (hopefully) lucrative for those wise enough to deploy their strategies."

Lou Kerner, Partner Flight Ventures

"As a general partner at a venture capital firm, I see the trends laid out in *Build Your Fortune in the Fifth Era* play out in my day job. This book provides an excellent primer for those who don't have the same vantage point."

Jeremy Liew, Partner Lightspeed Ventures

"A clear vision of how best to access, engage and profit from the wealth creation opportunities all around us, unfolding before our eyes. Technology innovation is the gold rush of our time on a global scale, and Matthew and Alison want each reader to find their own way to participate in and benefit from this wealth creation."

Nathan McDonald, Chairman Keiretsu Forum Northwest,
Partner Keiretsu Capital

"*Build Your Fortune in the Fifth Era* is a must read for any investor who wants to think differently about asset allocation. With the massive changes in the markets that Matthew and Alison reveal in this important book, financial advisers and savvy (accredited) investors alike would be wise to consider an asset allocation model that includes exposure to today's fastest-growing privately financed companies. This book provides a 'how to' roadmap along with important historical facts and enlightening supporting data."

Ned Montenecourt, Former Chief Compliance Officer
BlackRock Investments

"Investing in young companies is a hazardous undertaking where most participants lose. This book suggests ways to avoid that fate."

Michael Moritz, Partner Sequoia Capital

"*Build Your Fortune in the Fifth Era* lays out a roadmap for how this era is following patterns we've seen in previous disruptions. It's a great way to visualize the future both as an investor and entrepreneur, and find opportunities others will miss."

Gil Penchina, Partner at Flight Ventures,
Co-Founder of Fastly, 1 Angel on AngelList

"People are constantly asking me questions about angel investing and venture capital. Read this book if you want to understand the capital that fuels the entrepreneurs and technology innovation changing the world."

Keith Rabois, General Partner Khosla Ventures

"The best insight into the future comes from understanding the past. Tools and technologies evolve, but humans, as social animals, adapt to change in predictable ways. This book provides a deep grounding in where we came from, and where we are headed."

Jim Robinson, Managing Partner RRE Ventures

"The authors of *Build Your Fortune in the Fifth Era* generously share their experience, common sense and apparent sixth sense in concisely describing these rapidly changing technological times in which we live – the 'Fifth Era.' Their insightful advice on where and how to get ahead of the crowd as an entrepreneur, investor or employee is invaluable. Anyone interested in augmenting their future prosperity will be wise to understand and apply the intelligent perspectives of this book and, as a result, be positioned to attain abundant returns."

Ira P. Rothken, Founder Techfirm.com, Angel Investor

"*Build Your Fortune in the Fifth Era* reviews who made a disproportionate impact and reaped a disproportionate reward in previous economic eras, and hence lays the groundwork for looking at the current era and predicting the same thing for you: how as an angel investor, entrepreneur, passive fund investor, or in various other roles, you can impact and benefit from the world as it is now and is going to become."

Ian Sobieski, Ph.D., Chairman/Managing Member
Band of Angels, LLC

"*Build Your Fortune in the Fifth Era* provides an eye-awakening description of how technology today is changing our lives and creating new opportunities for wealth creation. No one can read this book and not be left struck by the uniqueness of our time, the potential for wealth creation, and the importance of embracing change."

Eric Stang, Chairman/CEO Ooma

"We are in the Fifth Era where there are exciting new ways of raising capital, and building wealth by accessing investment opportunities in new asset classes that are uncorrelated with existing choices. Fintech is transforming everything between the consumers of capital and those who seek alternative investments. This book provides a roadmap to navigate and prosper in the Fifth Era."

Denise Thomas, Founder/CEO ApplePie Capital

"Today's most valuable companies are built in the spirit of entrepreneurialism and technological innovation. And much of the value creation occurs before the companies go public, which means that most investors are not participating in this unprecedented wealth creation cycle. The authors clearly and simply outline ways to engage in this new 'Fifth Era,' from active investing and entrepreneurship to crowdfunding and passive investing."

Allan Thygesen, President Americas Google, Lecturer
Stanford Graduate School of Business

"A must-read and insightful book for those interested in understanding the world of technology and how to profit from it, written in easy-to-understand language by consummate Silicon Valley insiders Matthew Le Merle and Alison Davis. It is also very much a practical self-help book to get you into the technology game. As a UK-based investor from another part of the world, I found it particularly useful to gain insight as to what really is happening in the Bay Area technology space and how to profit from it going forward."

Julian Treger, Executive Director/CEO Anglo Pacific

"*Build Your Fortune in the Fifth Era* is a timely and important read. Alison and Matthew share their deep and broad experience to encourage broader participation in the investment opportunity that is one of the most unique, and potentially rewarding, of our lifetime."

Tracey Brophy Warson, North America Private Banking Head

"The rate of change in society over the past five years has been staggering, and the next five years promises even greater change. More clearly than any other source I have seen, *Build Your Fortune in the Fifth Era* describes in detail how to participate in, and profit from this change as an entrepreneur and/or an investor."

Colin Wiel, Founder/Co-CEO Mynd, Angel Investor

"This inspirational 'must read' gives you a lens into the world of start-ups and the critical and seminal role angels play. There is great risk...and greater opportunity ahead for you if you challenge yourself to learn and grow from the knowledge and expertise of the authors. Dive in...It will change your life. It has mine..."

Randy Williams, Founder/CEO/Partner Keiretsu Forum/Capital

"Matthew and Alison provide a large number of insights and perspectives that will be invaluable to potential investors and entrepreneurs. This book is required reading if you're serious about being more than simply lucky."

Rob Wiltbank, CEO Galois, Inc.

"If you want to understand what the future opportunities are in our technology driven world, you need to read this book. It would take most people more than 20 years to learn what this book explains in an afternoon of reading."

James Zhang, CEO Concept Art House,
Entrepreneur and Investor

BUILD YOUR FORTUNE
IN THE
FIFTH ERA

Also by Matthew C. Le Merle and Alison Davis

Corporate Innovation in the Fifth Era

BUILD YOUR FORTUNE

IN THE

FIFTH ERA

How to Prosper in an Age
of Unprecedented Innovation

MATTHEW C. LE MERLE
AND ALISON DAVIS

FIFTH
ERA
Focused on Innovation

First Printing 2017

ISBN: 978-0-9861613-3-9 (Amazon paperback)
ISBN: 978-0-9861613-4-6 (hardbound)
ISBN: 978-0-9861613-5-3 (paperback)

Library of Congress Cataloging-in-Publication Data is available.

This work was designed and printed in the United States of America by

CARTWRIGHT
PUBLISHING
Visibility • Authority • Legacy • Clients

145 Corte Madera Town Center, #415
Corte Madera, CA 94924

www.CartwrightPublishing.com
415-250-6343

Cartwright Publishing is a publisher of business and professional books. We help entrepreneurs, business leaders and professionals share their stories, passion and knowledge to help others. If you have a manuscript or book idea that you would like us to consider for publishing, please visit CartwrightPublishing.com

Cover photo: Matthew Le Merle
Cover design: Katherine Masters
Interior design: Sue Balcer

For Maximillian, Tallulah, Louis, Felix and Leonardo.
May you prosper and make your mark in the Fifth Era

Free Updates and Bonus Content!

Visit <u>BuildYourFortuneintheFifthEra.com</u>
To receive free book updates, additional content about the topics
covered in this book, and find out more about the authors.

A Note from the Authors

Part 1 of this book has been included in its entirety in our companion work:

Corporate Innovation in the Fifth Era

For those of our readers who have read this book,
we recommend you proceed to Part 2.

Table of Contents

Table of Exhibits

Table of Sidebars

Introduction

The beginning is the most important part of the work.

—Plato

It was November 2006, and we had been invited to speak to representatives of the 34 provinces of China in the Great Hall of the people in Tiananmen Square. The express purpose of the invitation from the Chinese government was for us to "teach the people of China how to be angel investors." We, and a delegation from Keiretsu Forum, the world's largest angel network, had flown to Beijing to respond properly to this request.

Looking out across the hall filled with Chinese provincial representatives in suits, it was a little intimidating. Though this was one of the smaller meeting spaces, it was still a large room, so there would be little dialogue with the audience: a handful of slides on a massive screen; the speech; perhaps a few questions; all translated simultaneously. As far as we could see people were donning their headphones and looking up in anticipation.

Over the next 30 minutes we gave a similar talk to one we had given a number of times to government delegations from other countries visiting San Francisco and California – China, France, Germany, Korea, India, the UK and others – and also to teams of leaders from multinational companies, that had come to learn the lessons of Silicon Valley and how to drive innovation in their home countries and companies. Sometimes we spoke as representatives of Fifth Era, our investment and advisory firm. Sometimes as representatives of the State of California or Bay Area Council—Northern California's leading economic development partnership. Sometimes as partners of a management consulting firm. Sometimes, like today, as angel investors and members of the world's largest angel organization.

The storyline was as follows. Disruptive innovations are changing the world and moving it into a new era that is unlike anything we have experienced before—we define it as the "Fifth Era." Every industry is being impacted, and life as we know it on the planet will change significantly. Clusters of innovation are arising in certain regions and cities, and creating geographic hubs for the disruptive companies and innovators.

After outlining the components of a cluster of innovation, we then leave the audience with the punchline—all of this great period of disruption is being driven by a small number of people in two groups: the technology entrepreneurs and the angels who are backing them. But neither of these groups is sufficiently understood and supported. First, the technology entrepreneurs are very few in number and are able to be based anywhere they want to be. So, to attract and retain them they need careful cultivation and support. Secondly, the people who back them are the unsung angel investors who write the first checks. Every prospective innovation hub needs to focus on creating and motivating these angels in order to have companies that venture capitalists may eventually want to back. But without the angel investors, the whole innovation machine not only does not get primed—it never gets started.

In 2006, at the end of our speech in Tiananmen Square, we were asked only three questions by the Chinese representatives. The first: "What is an angel investor?" The second: "Why do they want to invest in early-stage companies?" And the third: "What should we do in China—we don't have any angel investors?"

In the decade since that talk, we have returned to China many times and been quite involved in assisting Shanghai and the Yangtze River region expand its innovation clusters in industries, like IT, ecommerce, digital entertainment, and biotechnology, and in industrial parks, like Zhangjiang Hi-Tech Park in Pudong and the Knowledge Innovation Center of Yangpu.

On our most recent trip in 2016, we were discussing just how much had changed since that earlier trip in 2006. Now China is full of innovation hubs, technology parks, incubators, and accelerators of all shapes and sizes. There are abundant sources of capital, including from angels, angel groups, micro-venture capital funds, large-scale venture capital funds, and other entities expressly created to channel capital into innovative hands. As you travel through the provinces and major cities of China it seems as if every Chinese local government has the same strategy: to build a leading innovation cluster in a new city within, or attached to, the old city. And their collective objective is to make the new innovation clusters competitive with other places around the world, including Silicon Valley. Always in the same areas of disruptive innovation: the Internet, cloud computing, big data and artificial intelligence, robotics, augmented reality/virtual reality (AR/VR), the Internet of things (IOT), biotechnology, clean energy, blockchain technology, and others.

Between 2006 and 2016, it seemed as if every city in China learned how to harness disruptive innovations and was seeking to play in a global game. In every city we met affluent Chinese who were investing behind these strategies, either on their own accounts or in partnership with their local government leaders—with the express intent of building their family a fortune.

The change was very substantial and very evident to someone who visited from time to time and could see the changes over the timeframe of a year or two. Sometimes when you are in the middle of change, it is hard to see it taking place.

On returning from our most recent trip we took stock of the ten years of change. We noted the new nature of our conversations and the much more precise and targeted questions we are now asked by Chinese government officials who have moved far beyond those first three questions in the Great Hall of the People.

Then, a funny thing happened . . .

We landed back in the US, somewhat jetlagged, and the next day we were scheduled for two meetings. One, to meet a delegation of local state officials from two Midwestern states who were interested in bringing more of Silicon Valley innovation to their respective markets—major Midwestern cities. Two, at the request of the UK government, to meet a delegation from Northern England who had the same objective.

We gave our comments and then offered to answer their questions. And in each case the first three questions were along the lines of: "What is an angel investor?" "Why do they want to invest in early-stage companies?" and "What should we do—we don't have any angel investors?"

And it suddenly struck us—

While we have been traveling to the other side of the world, helping China drive its innovation agenda, we have taken it for granted that everyone in the US and Europe is informed and moving forward and participating in the disruptive innovations of our time.

For more than 30 years we have lived and worked in the US and in Silicon Valley, first coming from England to attend Harvard and Stanford Universities, then working as management consultants at McKinsey & Company, AT Kearney, Monitor Group, and Booz & Company. We took on senior executive roles at the well-known retailer Gap as SVP strategy and marketing; and at the world's largest institutional investment firm, Barclays Global Investors (now Blackrock) as chief financial officer. We spent time as venture partner and private equity partner at Monitor Ventures and Belvedere Capital, respectively. Then, over a twenty-year timeframe, we transitioned to being angel investors and board directors with public and private companies.

During those years, we became immersed in innovation and entrepreneurialism. We helped corporations become better at innovation, invested in and supported start-ups launching disruptive businesses, and advised countries and regions on how to be more in the flow of innovation. We have been immersed in the disruptions of our time and in the new digital world that is being built around us, and because we are in the middle of this changing world, we take much of it for granted.

But, that is not true for most people in the US or in most countries around the world. As we will show in this book, in the US, for example, of the 12.5 million households that could be accredited investors in early-stage technology companies, less than 3% are actually investing in these companies today. Ninety-seven percent of those that could are not participating in the greatest wealth-creation opportunity the world has ever seen.

For most people, this most important of times is passing them by. The world is transitioning between two eras—from the Industrial Era that we have grown up in, into the Fifth Era of digital and biotechnology disruption and change—and most people are not sure how to participate.

They don't know the options for playing or how to go about building their fortunes in this time of transition.

Most people are on the sidelines of a game, watching, while only vaguely aware of the rules of play.

We have written this book for everyone around the world who is aware that we are living in a time of transition between eras but does not have a clear strategy for participating.

This book outlines the nature of the change the world is in the middle of, describes many of the disruptive innovations and the impact they are having, shows why this is the greatest phase of wealth creation the world has ever seen, and provides options and a decision-making process that will allow every reader to choose how to play—or will at least make them more informed if they make the decision not to.

We hope that through this book we effectively share content that has, in a modest way, contributed to major steps forward in those places where we have shared it already. We want to share that knowledge with everyone who is interested in learning more. We have written this book for an international audience, but given our own experience and expertise, most of our facts, sources, and case studies are US ones. Please accept our apologies that we don't have as many international examples as we would like; conversely, we still believe that the contents of this book are as important internationally as they are here in the US where we live and work. And we are sure that the options presented are the right ones for people in most countries around the world. Having visited four continents to share these insights during the last three years, we can confirm that local audiences have told us so.

We believe that the world needs the active participation of many more people—as innovators, entrepreneurs, and investors—if we are to harness the power of disruptive innovations to make the future a better one for ourselves and our children. And if you make a fortune in the process, what can be wrong with that?

Good luck as you build your fortune in the Fifth Era.

Matthew C. Le Merle
Alison Davis
Tiburon, California, USA

Part 1 | The Fifth Era

Chapter 1
Past Is Prologue – First Four Eras

Study the past if you would divine the future.

—Confucius

Decades ago, few would have been able to imagine just how different the world would be today. Three decades ago, we were largely unconnected from one another. It took time to create, share, or find data and content, and we relied upon physical means to do so. To innovate, manufacture, market, and distribute their products companies and industries relied upon approaches that had, in some cases, gone unchanged for many decades. Information was to be found in libraries, archives, and desk drawers, if you knew where to look.

In just 30 years, all of that has changed.

Today, we are connected, information is broadly available and easy to find, innovation is quick and iterative, and innovators are able to access the latest technologies and tools wherever they are across the globe. Today, most companies conduct their businesses in fundamentally different ways, providing cheaper, better, and faster products to their customers, and this is only the beginning. As new technologies continue to emerge and innovation continues to disrupt, we will build upon the foundations, laid out just three decades ago with the creation of the Internet and the digital economy, to launch ourselves into a Fifth Era of economic activity.

In order to better understand just how dramatically different this Fifth Era might be, we think that it is worthwhile to begin this book by briefly reviewing the four eras of human activity that have gone before to see how disruptive innovations were able to change the very essence of human activity around the world and the opportunities that this created for new wealth creation.

While each of the four eras of human activity was very different in nature, there are some common themes that will be relevant as we look at the coming Fifth Era. First, that disruptive innovations are able to fundamentally change the essence of the way that most people spend their time. Second, that new and very different wealth-creation opportunities surface as human activity adjusts to the new era and the activities that characterize it. Third, that this wealth creation does not automatically accrue to the best-positioned and most successful players of the prior era. And finally, that it is possible to see a new era coming and position yourself for the next phase of wealth creation, but that this has to be a distinct choice: prior wealth-creation strategies may not be relevant in the subsequent era.

The four eras that we will briefly cover are the **Hunter-Gatherer Era**, which began in times long past—perhaps 2.5 million years ago—and began to give way to the next era between 12,000 and 11,000 years ago. As with other subsequent eras, we still see vestiges of foraging societies in remote parts of the world today. However, the vast majority of humans have moved on into other ways of spending their time. We will then briefly look at the **Agrarian Era**, which began about 11,000 years ago and continued roughly until the beginning of the fifteenth century AD. We will then turn to the **Mercantile Era**, which came to be the dominant economic mode between 1400 and 1800 when the world became, for the first time, a connected trading environment. Finally, we will review the **Industrial Era**, which was launched with the first industrial revolution in the mid-nineteenth century and passed through three distinct phases culminating in today's industrialized world.

While there is a great deal of overlap between these four eras, and in each subsequent era some peoples and groups continued to live by the rules of the prior era(s), nonetheless, the center of gravity and the driving force of human society is quite distinct in each era. So today, we still see foragers in the rainforest and tundra, agrarian communities on most continents, and mercantile traders everywhere—but the dominant theme of the last two centuries has been that of an industrialized world.

Each of these four eras was supplanted by dramatic innovations that enabled society to move into a new phase of existence, and it is these disruptive innovations that we are beginning to see surfacing at an increasingly rapid rate, giving us confidence that the fourth era is beginning to close and the Fifth Era is about to arrive. However, the time of transition between eras can be measured in generations and is always messy—we are living in the time of transition between the Industrial and Fifth Eras today, and no one can be sure exactly what the future will hold. What we can be sure of is that the Fifth Era will create exciting new wealth-creation opportunities just as each new era did in times past.

Exhibit 1
The Five Eras

Era	Name	Span	Distruptive Innovations
1	Hunter/ Gatherer	— to 11,000 BC	—
2	Agrarian	11,000 BC to ±1400 AD	• Domestication —First high productivity crops — Local Animal Husbandry • Irrigation • Farming Tools • Storage
3	Mercantile	±1400 AD to ±1800 AD	• Great global convergence and new forms of transportation • Columbian exchange of plants and animals • Global economy with common forms of currency and methods of exchange
4	Industrial	±1800 AD to ±2000 AD	INITIALLY • Steam Engine • Blast Furnaces • Early machine tools THEN • Electricity • Steel FINALLY • Computers
5	Fifth Era	±2000 AD	• Digital Revolution • Biotechnology • Others

Source: Fifth Era, LLC

The Hunter-Gatherer Era

From the ancient past up until about 11,000 or 12,000 years ago, most people on the face of the earth lived by hunting and gathering in a subsistence economy. Some researchers also call this the Forager Era, and there are groups of people who still rely upon this way of living today. In the ancient past, people lived by gathering and collecting the abundance of nature: hunting and trapping big and small game, fishing and gathering shellfish, and making use of whatever plant foods they could find. Most hunters and gatherers combined these various types of food acquisition. They varied their forms of foraging depending upon the seasons, the movements and availability of animals, and the natural cycles of harvesting opportunities.

Most of these hunter-gatherer cultures were close to subsistence communities, and typically only small surpluses could be gathered and saved for periods of scarcity. Certain plants could be kept without spoiling, some animal products might be dried and stored, but for the most part, the community relied upon the availability of the moment.

Throughout this first era the dominant societal mode was a tribal group—a band of people who would collaborate, work together, and help each other—often tied together by blood in extended family groups. Typically, they would rely upon the local environment for their needs, and if they did exhaust the local environment, they might need to be nomadic, either on a continuous or an episodic basis. Groups were small in number, typically 100 or less, and there was very little ability to create permanent settlements. Continuous foraging in the same space was rarely feasible, so settlements would be periodically abandoned in all but the most fruitful places.

Whether you subscribe to Thomas Hobbes' view of 1651, that the lives of hunter-gathers were "solitary, poor, nasty, brutish and short" or prefer the view that Marshall Sahlins proffered in the 1960s, that, rather, they were the "original affluent society" with most of their time reserved for leisure, what is sure is that they were unable to accumulate much in the way of material wealth. Wealth creation was limited with most individuals being active foragers in a small-group setting. Few were able to accumulate significantly more than the average of their group—leaders of groups might accumulate more spare time by asking others to forage on their behalf and might share a disproportionate part of the group's possessions. But, to a large extent, accumulation of wealth was not possible.

During this era, the world's population grew to perhaps 4 million by the arrival of the second great era.

No surpluses meant no accumulation of material wealth in the hands of the rich.

The Agrarian Era

Some 11,000 years ago we see the widespread arrival of a new Agrarian Era. While some limited farming had certainly existed for thousands of years before, in a relatively short timeframe of a few thousand years we see the appearance of farming as the dominant paradigm on almost every continent with the exception of Australia. And while some peoples continued to hunt and gather, the majority became dependent upon planned agricultural activities for most of their needs.

The disruptive innovations that displaced foraging with agriculture were created as the result of some thousands of years of experimentation as farmers sought to improve the yields they could produce from the land they tended. They did this by creating more productive and reliable crops and breeding more productive animals, thus becoming ever better at domestication. They created better and better tools with which to farm, and they learned the essentials of irrigation, mass harvesting, and the storing of their surplus produce. The combination of many individual innovations drove the Agrarian Era forward.

The first major period of disruptive change that we have record of is the so-called First Agricultural Revolution, which is also named the Neolithic Revolution after historian V. Gordon Childe (1929). This was a period, particularly in the Middle East, when animal husbandry and crop farming techniques reached a point of development that, when combined with better irrigation technologies, allowed for much higher yields and much higher density of population. In those parts of the world impacted, foraging was largely displaced by settled agrarian communities that then focused on further improving their farming technologies and practices.

A Second Agricultural Revolution, or a Medieval Green Revolution, began around the eighth century in the Islamic world, where very high-producing crops appear to have emerged for the first time, including wheat, rice, cotton, and sorghum (Watson, A.M., 1974). Again, with the help of irrigation, these four staple crops appear to have dramatically changed the way that society progressed and also, for the first time, gave the opportunity for people to accumulate wealth, primarily through the ownership of land and the leadership of communities.

The second agrarian phase saw the beginning of the rise of large, well-organized empires. In particular, the three largest of the period between 1000 BC and 500 AD: the Persian Achaemenid Empire, the Han Empire in China, and the Roman Empire. These empires also became the locus for wealth capture driven by their ruling elites, however they rose to power.

These three, and many other smaller empires, developed powerful military forces and mercantile and trading skills to expand their reach and to influence other agrarian people to support their expansion. The vast majority of people living in this period were living on the land as farmers, however, the existence of soldiers, merchants, traders, and other specialized service providers became widespread.

Fueled by these disruptive agrarian innovations, the population of the world began to increase rapidly—from perhaps 4 million some 11,000 years ago to around 450 million at the end of the second era in 1400.

Exhibit 2

World Population Curve

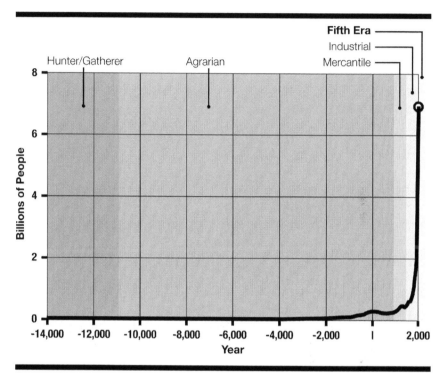

Source: United Nations Data Sheet, 2016; Fifth Era, LLC

In Europe, a final phase of the Agrarian Era began in the eighteenth century by which time the Mercantile Era was firmly established. The enclosing of the commons, the arrival of new techniques for planting and harvesting crops, and the continuing rollout of new crop rotation, irrigation, and stock-breeding technologies greatly increased farming productivity. The concentration of the ownership of land in this time-frame gave rise to very significant wealth creation fixed in the hands of the European landed gentry.

However, by then most nations had discovered a much more productive way to focus their efforts: the Mercantile Era.

The Mercantile Era

In the Agrarian Era, the primary locus of wealth creation was the ownership of land and the control of the surpluses that that land was yielding. By the Mercantile Era, which begins around 1400, we see much more emphasis on trade and wealth being created by those that were able to participate in and control the exchange of goods around the world.

The disruptive innovations of this period that ushered in the new era were threefold. First, we see the great global convergence in which new and sophisticated transportation and communication approaches linked every continent. The age of sail allowed long-distance trading to take place on the world's oceans and the great sea-trading nations—England, France, Holland, Portugal, and Spain, among others—rose to prominence and their merchants and sovereigns accumulated great wealth.

This great global convergence, in turn, gave rise to the second disruptive innovation of this period—the Columbian exchange of plants, animals, and microorganisms between continents. In a very short period of time, the breakthrough innovations of domestication that had taken place in an unlinked fashion in the thousands of years before were suddenly shared. The Europeans got the potato and corn (maize), the Americans got the goat and wheat, and so on. In every part of the world, great increases in productivity occurred—although destructive microorganisms and diseases were also shared to the detriment of some societies, especially in the Americas.

The combination of these two great innovations led to the third breakthrough innovation of the Mercantile Era—the creation of a global economy with common forms of currency and accepted ways to exchange goods in marketplaces. Silver and gold became widely accepted, and the merchants and merchant houses scoured the world for opportunities to buy low and sell high, moving goods at great risk between the sellers and the buyers that they connected. With the help of large sailing vessels they could do this at scale—not just the goods that could be packed on the backs of a camel caravan or ox-pulled cart.

Adam Smith (1776) coined the term "mercantile system" to

describe how the early mercantile states worked to enrich themselves by restricting imports while working to expand their exports. This created a favorable balance of trade that would bring gold and silver into the state to the benefit of the mercantile elites. Following this pattern, Europe, in particular, saw the creation of wealthy trading cities and powerful organizations, such as the East India Company.

The Mercantile Era also saw the creation of military power on a scale not seen before as trading nations sought to secure their trading routes and extend their influence over the endpoints of their trading networks. The rise of the scientific method during the Scientific Revolution and the Enlightenment of this Mercantile Era also laid the groundwork for the coming Industrial Era. Science was now able to move faster than ever without the constraints of religious and political beliefs that had before made experimentation and innovation often hazardous to the health of the innovator. Just as the Mercantile Era saw the global trading of goods, it also saw a first global exchange of ideas.

The world's population grew from some 450 million to 1.3 billion by 1800, the next major time of transition.

The wealth creation of the Mercantile Era did not accrue automatically to those societies and leaders who had risen to prominence in the Agrarian Era. Indeed, the great empires of Asia, the Middle East, and to some extent the Americas were slow to adjust to the realities of the Mercantile Era and the need to master new transportation and trading innovations. Instead, the wealth creation of the era went to those who moved quickly to master these new innovations—the new merchants and merchant states.

The Industrial Era

The Industrial Era is the fourth era that we will review, beginning in the mid-eighteenth century and bringing us to today. The Industrial Era has passed through three distinct phases, each of which illustrates our core theme—disruptive innovations drive us forward and in so doing produce great wealth-creation opportunities for those who choose to master the new realities.

The first phase of disruption within the Industrial Era was the great Industrial Revolution of the mid-eighteenth century. Disruptive innovations, like the spinning jenny and spinning mule in textiles, the stationary steam engine, the blast furnace, and early machine tools, dramatically increased productivity. These early breakthroughs were accelerated by a shift in the types of energy that society used from biomass-based energy—primarily burning wood—to the age of coal and steam. These fossil fuels allowed much more efficient generation of energy and, with the invention and continuous development of the steam engine, allowed human beings to become much more effective in the ways that they created products and services. The steam engine was used to power machinery across almost every manufacturing sector, allowing faster production of greater quantities of merchandise.

This first Industrial Revolution also saw the creation of the factory and workhouse, and it was not without opposition—Ned Ludd and his Luddites being foremost in opposing the application of disruptive technologies in this new Industrial Era.

This first phase of the Industrial Era was accompanied by a very substantial increase in world population that had been building during the Mercantile Era. By the end of the nineteenth century, the world's population was approaching two billion people. So, the Industrial Revolution saw a compounding of factors—a much larger world population and a fundamental transformation in the way that those people worked, produced, and lived.

The wealth creation of this period was primarily captured by the early industrialists and by those who applied new steam-based manufacturing approaches to existing industries, displacing manpower with machine power. These new manufacturing businesses were capital-intensive and, in many cases, family-owned businesses that needed additional capital influxes in order to compete. In this period we see the rise to supremacy of the corporate model of business, with companies owned by groups of shareholders raising capital from public markets and deploying it into expanding their operations. This is the model that continues as the dominant model in most places today.

The second phase of the Industrial Era, beginning around 1850, was driven by three new disruptive innovations—the widespread use of steel assisted by the invention of new mass steel furnaces by Sir Henry Bessemer, the arrival of electrical power, and the invention of mass production approaches beginning to be deployed at scale after the Great War (WW1). The corporate model continued to expand as more and more capital became available through the public markets. The development of national corporate champions then gave way in the mid-twentieth century to the development of multinational companies, capturing economies of scale and scope to dominate their target industries.

Despite two world wars and many smaller wars, the Industrial Era moved forward, and the world population continued to grow rapidly.

During the second half of the twentieth century, a large proportion of business activity was organized and managed within the four walls of the large public corporations. This is particularly true for innovation, where, beginning perhaps 100 years ago, corporate laboratories and R&D centers became increasingly important in driving innovations that would be utilized by the companies in their products and services.

The wealth creation of this timeframe was captured by corporate leaders and titans and by the financiers that backed them. Those who ran large corporations and those who played the capital financing games of the public markets captured most of the wealth creation of this phase.

The third major phase of the Industrial Era, termed the "Computer Age," is a result of the application of ever more powerful computing innovations to industrial activities. As we will show in the next section, we should make a clear distinction between the application of computing to established Industrial Era approaches and businesses versus the use of computing power to disrupt and replace these same businesses. In the Computer Age, as it applies to the third phase of the Industrial Era, the application of computer technologies to the activities of most large corporations around the world resulted in increases in their productivity.

However, computerization also unleashed a greatly increased rate of innovation and has enabled a new generation of innovators beyond the four walls of the industrial corporation. This has given rise to a new wave of disruptive innovations appearing at an accelerating pace, impacting every industry around the world.

In this era the world's population expanded rapidly from 1.3 billion in 1800 to today's 7.5 billion.

Divining the Future

Over the last tens of thousands of years, we have seen at least four distinct eras of human activity on the surface of the earth. These four eras, the Hunter-Gatherer Era, the Agrarian Era, the Mercantile Era, and the Industrial Era, all share common themes.

1. First, disruptive innovations are able to fundamentally change the essence of the way that most people spend their time.
2. Second, new and very different wealth-creation opportunities surface as human activity adjusts to the new era and the activities that characterize it.
3. Third, this wealth creation does not automatically accrue to the best-positioned and most successful players of the prior era.
4. And finally, it is possible to see a new era coming and position yourself for the next phase of wealth creation, but this has to be a distinct choice: prior wealth-creation strategies may not be relevant in the subsequent era.

This is why we say the past is prologue.

Today disruptive innovations are coming at an ever-increasing rate. They are fundamentally displacing the "paradigm" of the fourth Industrial Era. Thomas Kuhn explained in his famous 1962 treatise *The Structure of Scientific Revolutions* that scientific paradigm shifts occur when some recognized problem of science, which has not been solved before, not only can be solved within a new paradigm but that the new paradigm also is able to preserve a relatively large part of the problem-solving that has been accomplished in the prior paradigm. When a new paradigm is able to do this, a shift occurs.

Today the disruptive innovations are surfacing at an ever-increasing rate, which we will detail in the next chapter. They are not only solving heretofore fundamental challenges of the Industrial Era, but they are able to do so while also holding onto the progress of that Era. They are meeting, essentially, the test that Kuhn created but are doing so at the societal level, not just at the level of a scientific breakthrough.

As we seek to understand the Fifth Era, the words of Confucius that began this chapter are important: "Study the past if you would divine the future."

In the next chapter, we will catalog a sample of the new innovations and the disruptive impacts they represent. Then, in the third chapter, we will combine them and show how this is the arrival of a new era of human activity.

Chapter 2
Disruptive Innovation Ushering in a New Era

The historian of science may be tempted to exclaim that when paradigms change, the world itself changes with them.

—Thomas Kuhn

The transition from one era to another has always been initiated and driven by disruptive innovations that have enabled society to fundamentally change the focus of activity and have produced new beneficiaries of wealth creation. But, the time of transition between eras is not quick and straightforward. It is a messy period that may extend over generations and which sees false starts, dead ends, and may advance faster in one place than another. The time of transition is, however, a period of dramatic transformation and wealth creation.

Do all disruptive innovations transform society to the level of an era change? Far from it. Most disruptive innovations occur within the context of a specific era. They improve and change the practices of that era, but they don't push it into a new era. The process of disruptive innovation is continuous, and most innovations provide incremental changes, which move society forward but don't challenge the very nature of the era in which they are born and established.

So, as observers of innovation, how would we know if the disruptive innovations we are observing are sufficient to herald a transition in eras? How would we know if we were in the time of transition?

Let's take an empirical look at today's disruptive innovations and ask the question: "Are these innovations incremental, or are they so disruptive as to be the heralds of a time of transition between eras?" This chapter does this first by looking at the innovations of the second half of the Industrial Era, next by considering the most recent innovations of the last thirty years, and then by observing the next waves of innovations that are beginning to surface. The aim of this chapter is to answer that question by demonstrating that we are shifting into a very disruptive phase of innovation that heralds the arrival of an entirely new era: the Fifth Era.

19th Century Disruptive Innovations

In 1913, at the peak of the Industrial Era, *Scientific American* conducted a survey with their readers asking them for a list of "the greatest innovations of our time." The readers of the magazine were encouraged to write essays, making the case for particular innovations that should be on the list. Then *Scientific American* extracted the full list of candidate innovations from those essays, created a short list of the most mentioned, and called for a vote of all readers of the magazine. This master list of the greatest innovations of the time was published in 1913.

Exhibit 3
The Greatest Innovations of Our Time – 1913

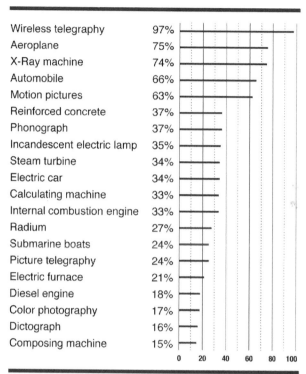

Wireless telegraphy	97%
Aeroplane	75%
X-Ray machine	74%
Automobile	66%
Motion pictures	63%
Reinforced concrete	37%
Phonograph	37%
Incandescent electric lamp	35%
Steam turbine	34%
Electric car	34%
Calculating machine	33%
Internal combustion engine	33%
Radium	27%
Submarine boats	24%
Picture telegraphy	24%
Electric furnace	21%
Diesel engine	18%
Color photography	17%
Dictograph	16%
Composing machine	15%

Source: *Scientific American*

In first place, we see wireless telegraphy was voted by 97% of *Scientific American* readers as being the top innovation. Next we see the airplane, X-ray machine, automobile, and so on.

The list is interesting in several ways. First, there was general agreement over which innovations were the most important in their time. The top five innovations were voted as the greatest by most voters, and then there is a significant drop-off as we reach the sixth innovation on the list: reinforced concrete. Secondly, many of the innovations are still central to our lives today—the airplane, X-ray machine, automobile, reinforced concrete, and incandescent electric lamp, to name just five. These innovations can be long-lived. Third, these innovations were very much characteristic of the Industrial Era at that time: they are almost all physical products that combine mechanical engineering with either fossil fuel or electrical energy sources, which is, of course, the defining essence of the Industrial Era itself.

The innovations on this list are disruptive, for sure, but they are not heralds of a disruption to the Industrial Era itself. *Scientific American* readers of 1913 were firmly in the middle of the Industrial Era—they were not living in a time of transition between eras.

20th Century Disruptive Innovations

Let us now look at the same question being asked *by Forbes Magazine* and The Wharton School in 2009. This time Forbes and Wharton asked readers to list "the top innovations of the prior 30 years" from 1979 through to 2009.

Exhibit 4

Forbes List of the Top Innovations of the Prior 30 years – 2009

1. Internet, broadband, www
2. PC/laptop computers
3. Mobile phones
4. E-mail
5. DNA testing and sequencing/human genome mapping
6. Magnetic Resonance Imaging (MRI)
7. Microprocessors
8. Fiber optics
9. Office software (spreadsheets, word processors)
10. Non-invasive laser/robotic surgery (laparoscopy)
11. Open-source software and services
12. Light-emitting diodes
13. Liquid crystal display (LCD)
14. GPS systems
15. Online shopping/e-commerce/auctions
16. Media file compression (jpeg, mpeg, mp3)
17. Microfinance
18. Photovoltaic solar energy
19. Large- scale wind turbines
20. Social networking via the Internet

Source: *Forbes Magazine* and The Wharton School, 2009

This list is very different from the list created in 1913. In 2009, some of the innovations are physical products just as they were in 1913—PC/laptop computers, mobile phones, MRI machines, and so on. But, more of the innovations are no longer physical at all—they are virtual innovations—the Internet, e-mail, various forms of software, and the activities the software enables, such as online shopping, social networking, and so on. Also, we have on this list the first of the major biotechnology breakthroughs: DNA testing and sequencing, and human genome mapping.

This list of the top innovations of the end of the twentieth century is shaped by two "mega" disruptive innovations—the Digital Revolution and the Biotechnology Revolution. The innovations mostly rest upon digital technologies. Many of them are virtual in nature, and in the case of breakthroughs in the life sciences, they focus on a better understanding and the engineering of life itself and of humankind.

The question to ask at this juncture is "Are these innovations of the last 30 years evolutionary and incremental within the context of the Industrial Era, or are they disruptive and so different from the innovations of the Industrial Era that they are heralds of a new era, the Fifth Era?"

We have concluded the latter, and expect that many of you are already convinced. But, for those who are unsure or who wish to argue that this is just another phase in the evolution of the Industrial Era, let's keep going and look at the next wave of disruptive innovations of the twenty-first century. In order to better explore the coming wave of disruptive innovations, let us first explore the two mega disruptive innovations of our time—the Digital Revolution and the Biotechnology Revolution.

The Digital Revolution

The Digital Revolution can be thought of as the time in which physical, mechanical innovations gave up their centrality in human life to virtual, digital innovations. Central among these—and the disruptive innovation that did the most to connect all human beings into one digitally connected entity—is the Internet. The Internet was invented by a handful of scientists as a resource for scientists. However, today, it has grown to become an essential instrument for more than four billion users worldwide.

Today, most industry sectors are being substantially transformed by this rapid and unprecedented expansion. For example, music, video, software, news, books, and even money markets are being re-shaped because of the Internet. Human interactions have taken on a new nature as individuals use the Internet to gather information, educate themselves, go about their work, network socially, and entertain themselves and others. These changes are present and relevant in every region of the world, making the Internet a truly global and increasingly influential phenomenon.

Exhibit 5
Internet Penetration by Region

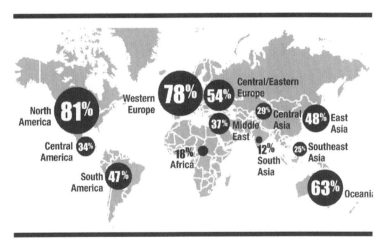

Sources: US Census Bureau, InternetWorldStats, CNNIC, Tencent, Facebook, ITU, CIAI, Fifth Era, LLC

While the process of change generated by the growth of the Internet and the emergence of new technologies has been swift and sweeping, it's far from complete. Substantial benefits are still to be captured. In this regard, the Digital Revolution is at the beginning rather than the end of its course. The Internet creates a tremendous amount of value for the global economy, substantially impacting GDP in most countries.

Exhibit 6

Internet Economy as a Percentage of 2016 GDP

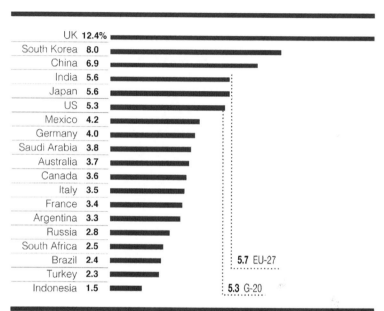

Sources: BCG Analysis; Economist Intelligence Unit; Organization for Economic Co-operation and Development (OECD), Fifth Era, LLC

In fact, the Internet contributes more to GDP than education and agriculture—two industries that are often highlighted in political decision-making.

Exhibit 7
Contribution of Selected Sectors to GDP

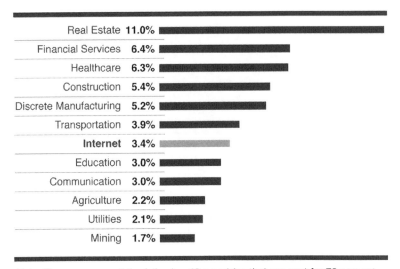

Note: Figures represent the following 13 countries that account for 70 percent of global GDP: Brazil, Canada, China, France, Germany, India, Italy, Japan, Russia, South Korea, Sweden, the United Kingdom, and the United States. Source: Organization for Economic Co-operation and Development (OECD), Fifth Era, LLC

Fast-emerging technologies are expected to continue to drive the Internet and its innovation. We have already seen cloud services and the mobile Internet allowing everything everywhere to be accessed in terms of content and data, and paving the way for new services and applications that are, today, widespread and used by most of us. The proliferation of faster access through 4G and new high-speed computing technologies are especially important as they've also enabled this data access and supported new social-networking approaches.

Exhibit 8
Social Technologies Penetration by Country

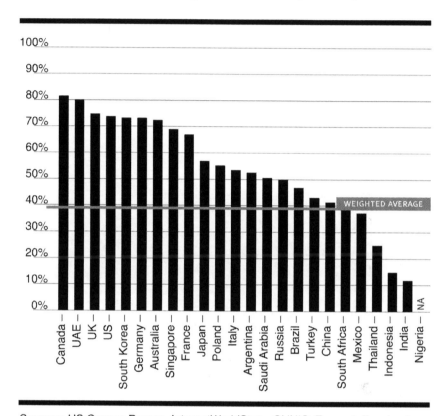

Sources: US Census Bureau, InternetWorldStats, CNNIC, Tencent, Facebook, ITU, CIA, Global Web Index, Fifth Era, LLC

The cloud, as well as more mobile connected devices, has also expanded such that the proportion of the global population covered by either mobile service or Internet access to at least 3G standards continues to expand rapidly. Today 3G is active in 181 countries and 4G in 63 countries, resulting in substantial increases in the penetration of the world's population by mobile devices.

Exhibit 9
Mobile Devices Penetration by Country

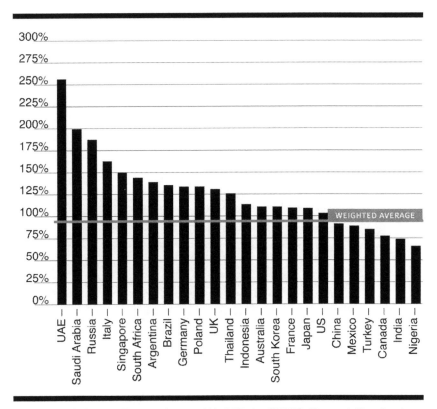

Sources: US Census Bureau, InternetWorldStats, CNNIC, Tencent, Facebook, ITU, CIA, Global Web Index, Fifth Era, LLC

Today it's inconceivable that we would be without the Internet, but just 30 years ago, it didn't even exist. This, as a disruptive influence, is unprecedented. In just a handful of years, we have gone from almost no Internet access for the majority of people, to upwards of four or five billion people incorporating it into their everyday life.

The Biotechnology Revolution

As explained in the first chapter of this book, for thousands of years, humankind used technology to engineer food production. During the Agrarian Era, we called this "domestication," and it was the process by which humans selected plants and animals, and emphasized in them the characteristics that they most valued and suppressed in them the characteristics that they no longer wanted to support. To a large extent, domestication was accomplished through multigenerational breeding of crops and animals in the direction that humans favored. Indeed, domestication was itself a disruptive innovation that took us into the Agrarian Era and has continued through today.

However, today's form of the domestication process—at the level of the gene—is fundamentally different from the processes of the past. The Biotechnology Revolution was ushered in by the fifth innovation listed on the 2009 *Forbes*/Wharton list: DNA testing and sequencing, and human genome mapping. These innovations allowed humans, for the first time, to look inside plants and animals, including human beings, and extend the process of domestication into engineering and evolving life itself.

In 2003 through 2005, my colleagues, Joan Chu and Nancy Michels, and I were invited by the State of California to develop a strategic action plan to ensure that the state's life sciences clusters remained at the forefront of the world's biotechnology revolution. To give some background, the term "cluster" refers to a geographic concentration of interconnected businesses, suppliers, and associated institutions in a particular field (Porter, 1998). Clusters are considered to increase the productivity with which companies can compete, nationally and globally. With that said, it makes sense the State of California wanted its life science clusters in the vanguard.

Working with the Monitor Group, a global strategy consulting firm, we developed a plan, which was widely accepted, that guided California's life sciences industry through a critical phase of development. The following synthesizes some of the findings of that work and continues to be true today, a decade later:

Since these initial breakthroughs and their acceleration through the creation of the Human Genome Project (HGP) in the 1980s, the Biotechnology Revolution has seen the emergence of new sub-technologies and subspecialties—entirely new areas of research unknown before. Proteomics, functional genomics, and bioinformatics are all examples of this HGP moving forward. This will continue to ratchet up as the demand for expertise in emerging areas of basic research are continued to ask for greater and new breakthroughs in the genome project. In the longer term, we are already beginning to see emerging technologies, such as gene therapy, stem cell research, and personalized medicine, also showing great promise for the continuing development of the life sciences industry globally.

Today, every one of us relies upon the innovation breakthroughs of this Biotechnology Revolution. The medicines that we are prescribed when we are sick are, more often than not, the results of recent genomic insights that have led to the creation of new drugs and treatments. The food that we eat has, to a large extent, been influenced by the same Biotechnology Revolution. While controversial, genetically modified organisms are very much in the food chain today, and continuing research emphasizes the prospect that they will be even more so in the future. The animals that we rely upon for our sources of protein have, to a lesser extent, been impacted by the Biotechnology Revolution. While we give them biotechnology-engineered foods and medicines, we have not to date engineered those animals to the extent that we now could—today's scientists know how to extend the process of domestication into engineering the genes of animals to better provide the characteristics that humans value. We have held back those scientists as society considers substantial questions about whether it supports this type of biotechnology-engineered animal livestock, but it's certainly something that we are already able to do—if we choose to do so. (Le Merle, M., Michels, N., & Chu, J., 2004)

The Biotechnology Revolution is the second major disruptive innovation of this transition period, and like the Digital Revolution, the resulting innovations stand in enormous contrast to the pre-existing medical technologies and innovations that were more common in the Industrial Era.

A Compounding of Innovations

Currently, the Digital Revolution and the Biotechnology Revolution are working together and compounding the impacts of each other. To date, this compounding has mostly moved in the direction of the Digital Revolution compounding the rate and impact of the Biotechnology Revolution. The former has allowed the ubiquitous availability of information, the speed and accessibility with which insights can be captured and shared, and the prospect of global collaboration between innovators and scientists to create new innovations together. We have seen remarkable rapid collaborative innovation to address global risks, such as severe acute respiratory syndrome (SARS) and Ebola, to name but two.

We are also seeing the flow of innovations beginning in the other direction as biotechnology (and chemistry and biology, more broadly defined) is beginning to be applied to new materials and approaches that may revolutionize computing and the Digital Revolution, just one example being the work on the organic chip and computer.

The Digital Revolution and the Biotechnology Revolution have already disrupted the global economy in dramatic ways, and they show the likelihood of even greater disruption in the future. But, they are only two of a number of emerging areas of disruptive innovation that we see transpiring today..

21st Century Disruptive Innovations

As we are writing this book in 2017, we see the emergence of a breadth of disruptive innovations more diverse than before, which offers the prospect of a plethora of specific inventions and breakthroughs. In 2016, we surveyed Keiretsu Forum (Sidebar 1: Keiretsu Forum and

Keiretsu Capital), the world's largest angel investor network and the most active early-stage venture investor in the US, asking investors across North America to predict what the most promising areas of innovation are likely to be, using a survey question that Sharespost had asked of its investor group: "Regardless of time horizons, where do you see the greatest growth opportunities in the future?"

Exhibit 10 shows the resulting ranking of areas of disruptive innovations as predicted by these active angel investors.

Exhibit 10

Ranking of Disruptive Innovation Areas

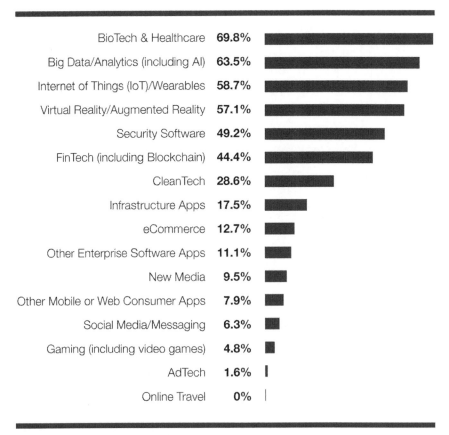

BioTech & Healthcare	**69.8%**
Big Data/Analytics (including AI)	**63.5%**
Internet of Things (IoT)/Wearables	**58.7%**
Virtual Reality/Augmented Reality	**57.1%**
Security Software	**49.2%**
FinTech (including Blockchain)	**44.4%**
CleanTech	**28.6%**
Infrastructure Apps	**17.5%**
eCommerce	**12.7%**
Other Enterprise Software Apps	**11.1%**
New Media	**9.5%**
Other Mobile or Web Consumer Apps	**7.9%**
Social Media/Messaging	**6.3%**
Gaming (including video games)	**4.8%**
AdTech	**1.6%**
Online Travel	**0%**

Sources: Keiretsu Capital, Fifth Era, LLC

Sidebar 1: Keiretsu Forum and Keiretsu Capital

We have been members and leaders of Keiretsu Forum and Keiretsu Capital for more than ten years, and many of the insights and opportunities that we describe in this book stem from that decade working with the other 2,500-plus angel investors that make up its membership.

Keiretsu Forum is a global investment community of accredited private equity angel investors, venture capitalists, and corporate/institutional investors. Keiretsu Forum was founded in the San Francisco East Bay in California in 2000 by Randy Williams. Keiretsu Forum is a worldwide network of capital, resources, and deal flow with 49 chapters on three continents. Keiretsu Forum members invest in high-quality, diverse investment opportunities. Keiretsu Forum and Keiretsu Capital (the exclusive worldwide fund partner of Keiretsu Forum) are ranked as the most active venture investors in the USA. The Keiretsu community is also strengthened through its involvement in social and charitable activities.

Exhibit 11
Most Active US Venture Investors, 2016

Most Active Investors Angel/Seed		Most Active Investors West Coast	
Firm	**Deals**	**Firm**	**Deals**
Keiretsu Forum	96	Keiretsu Forum	62
500 Startups	77	New Enterprise Associates	52
Innovation Works	25		
Y Combinator	24	Khosla Ventures	49
Indian Angel Network	23	Kleiner Perkins Caufield & Byers	42
Techstars	22	Andreessen Horowitz	41
Seedcamp	21	GV	37
SV Angel	21	SV Angel	34
Ben Franklin Technology Partners of Southeastern Pennsylvania	21	Y Combinator	34
		Accel Partners	33
SOSV	20	First Round Capital	32

Source: Pitchbook

> Between 2006 and 2009, we were actively leading the San Francisco and North Bay chapters of Keiretsu Forum. Since 2007 we have launched and led Keiretsu Capital and the angel co-investment funds that it operates along with our fellow general partners Nathan McDonald and Randy Williams.

In order to understand these new areas of disruptive innovation and to illustrate how they are giving rise to new business opportunities, let's briefly describe the top seven of these areas of disruptive innovations. We will also give examples of emerging growth companies that we have backed through the Keiretsu Capital Angel Co-Investment Funds, or the Fifth Era Digital Future Fund, an early-stage fund investing in digital disruptions in the digital commerce, digital content, and FinTech areas. These examples might be helpful for readers who want case studies to better expand their understanding of these technologies; we do not claim these examples are necessarily predictions of the most important companies of the future.

Biotechnology and Healthcare

We consider the Biotechnology Revolution to be one of the most important disruptive forces of the last 30 years of innovation, and we expect the rate of innovation in biotechnology to only increase and accelerate. We expect to see substantial and disruptive innovations in healthcare, agriculture and animal husbandry, and in other areas, like forestry, fishing, and so on, on a scale that we have never seen before. We also expect to see new innovations where biotechnology is applied to the digital economy, including in areas like organic computing.

Not surprisingly, there are a number of companies that we are investing in that are pushing the forefront of this space. Just as three examples: Embera is developing the first medication that treats addiction by moderating activity in the stress response system to reduce the cravings and loss of control that drive addiction. LumiThera is a developmental stage medical device company at the forefront in the development of photobiomodulation treatment protocols for age-related macular degeneration. Savara Pharmaceuticals is a US-based emerging pharmaceutical development company that is focused on advancing a pipeline of novel inhalation therapies for the treatment of patients with rare pulmonary conditions.

The synergies between biotechnology and information technology are already fueling innovation in many areas from the more traditional pharmaceutical, digital health, and agricultural industries to emerging industries, such as industrial biotechnology. We are seeing greater convergence in the form of cross-industry technologies and applications, like bioinformatics and nanotechnology. A move toward personalized healthcare and personalized medicine will continue as scientists leverage genomic information, massive computing power, and big data analysis to gain a more fundamental understanding of diseases, biological processes, and proteins that affect various disease states. Therapies developed by life sciences firms are creating high levels of specialization for targeted patient populations, and, indeed, biotechnologies enable us to develop many targeted drugs with diagnostic tests to determine a priori whether a drug will be effective for a particular patient's genomic profile.

Big Data, Analytics, and Applications of Artificial Intelligence (AI)

The Internet has already enabled content to be accessed by almost anyone in the world in real time and on demand so long as permissions are made available by the owners of the content. Computing power breakthroughs, including parallel computing, allow us to analyze much more content much more rapidly. Investors expect that future innovations around big data analytics will allow us to gather insights from larger and larger data sets. These data sets are becoming so large that we rely upon the computer itself to make sense of them. These are the first applications of artificial intelligence (AI). AI algorithms allow researchers to gain better insights and to make better decisions from ever-larger data sets, leveraging ever-greater computing power.

One example of an emerging company that we have backed that is operating in this space is Analyze. Analyze is an enterprise data, analytics, and software company based in Virginia. Analyze removes the friction between its clients and their data so that clients can surface actionable insights faster, leveraging their databases on 220 million US consumers and 360-plus unique data points on demographics, psychographic indicators, purchasing patterns, and more than 1 billion email addresses. Analyze is bringing AI and big data analytics to any consumer-facing company in any industry. A second example is DecisionNext, which is changing how companies do business in commodities-based industries. DecisionNext brings big data analytics to bear on commodities' sourcing and pricing decisions on behalf of its large corporate clients.

Of course, AI is not confined to helping make sense of data. AI holds the promise of making smart decisions too. In that regard it opens up the possibility that machines can take over many decisions that are, today, made by humans. In so doing, and when combined with innovations in robotics, this also allows for a future in which smart machines take over many tasks that humans want to be released from, as well as undertake new tasks that we cannot imagine today. Some examples include early experiments in self-steering or even self-driving vehicles, smart exoskeletons that allow the physically handicapped to move again as fully able people do, similar experiments that allow amplified speed, power, and duration in human activities, and robots that can go places and do things that humans can't, such as enter and work in heavily radioactive environments, like Fukushima, or harsh environments, like Mars, or dangerous environments, like unexploded mine and bomb situations in Afghanistan and Iraq, and so on.

The applications are almost limitless, and at their heart are the emerging companies that work in big data, analytics, and AI. This is why investors score this area so highly in their ranking.

Wearables and the Internet of Things (IoT)

The first Internet that we have all experienced to date is one that primarily connects computers and mobile devices together and allows us, as individuals, to gather content and to interact with each other through those computing devices. The next major push in terms of the endpoints is to create sensors that allow other devices (beyond our computers and mobile devices) to also be connected to the Internet.

These sensors allow, for example, a car or a refrigerator or a front door-bell to become a new connected endpoint of the Internet, and, in turn, this allows the Internet to extract information about the activities that these new endpoints are involved in. This "Internet of Things" (IoT) provides the promise that the devices we rely upon will one day be continuously monitored, enabling our service providers to take actions when they need to be fixed or replenished or replaced—though IoT holds the promise of much more than just these supporting activities.

Ooma is an IoT company that we work with at Fifth Era. Today, Ooma is a public company that is committed to transforming the landscape of home phone service and enabling the future of the digital home. At the center of their current offering is Ooma Office, an enterprise-level phone service for small businesses and Ooma Telo, a highly sophisticated computer that when connected to Ooma's cloud-based smart platform, delivers free calling with extremely high quality, advanced features, and connected services such that it turns any phone into a smartphone for your home.

Once IoT hubs, like Ooma, become established in offices and homes, they provide the potential to allow other less smart devices to be connected to the Internet, enabling the vision of a world of connected devices. Of course, the IoT is not just a home- or consumer-focused area of disruptive innovations. IoT is being extended into every industry and to every imaginable endpoint device. Examples include dispensing machines that know which sodas or snacks are most likely to need replenishment or what advertisements to show as users approach them at various times of the day. Another example is buildings that monitor who is in each room and whether heat, light, and sound should be adjusted, based upon occupancy and motion. There are technologies being deployed that monitor what parking spaces are used and provide the data to applications so that drivers don't endlessly circle, hoping to find a vacant space, but are, instead, directed in real time to slots as they open and close. And so on.

Wearables is the extension of this thought process to the clothes and the accessories that we carry with us everyday. Over the last couple of decades, most of us have supplemented our attire with a smart computing device that we used to think of as a phone, which, today, we think of as a powerful computer in a phone format: a smartphone. Wearables innovations take us to the next stage, potentially engineering the computing device and integrating it into accessories that we wear or even stitching it virtually throughout the clothes that we put on our bodies. Just as the IoT greatly expands the collection of and use of content from each of its endpoint devices, so the wearables movement could do the same for the wardrobes that we wear. One very novel company we have invested in is Textile-Based Delivery (Texdel), which has invented four patent-pending "platform" technologies that enable the secure and controlled delivery of "active" ingredients to a target location over a long period of time and through hundreds of laundering cycles. This means that apparel can be engineered to deliver vitamins, cosmetics, and even drugs to wearers over time. Examples might include driving gloves with caffeine in them, swimming costumes with built-in sunscreen, or even underwear that delivers needed vitamins.

Virtual Reality and Augmented Reality

In 1998, we were asked by the City of San Francisco and the Bay Area Council to create a strategic plan for the "multimedia industry" of the city to ensure that California would become the global leader in multimedia to add to its traditional leadership in the film industry by way of the Hollywood film cluster. Central to that strategy for San Francisco was the creation of a cluster that would combine digital technologies and the Internet with videogame content creation to form a new digital entertainment industry.

Over the last two decades since we created that plan, San Francisco and the Bay Area have become the world's leading digital entertainment cluster, and we have seen innovations in the ways that we access content and visualize and interact with information globally. In many industries, including entertainment, education, and military applications, we have sought to improve access devices that strive for even higher resolution and greater immersiveness through richer viewing experiences and better sound.

The next step in this continuing innovation around our access devices is expected to be in the areas of virtual reality (VR) and augmented reality (AR). Virtual reality enables participants to step into the content and be a part of it, whereas augmented reality allows participants to layer information on top of real-world images that they may be experiencing. Billions of dollars are being invested in both of these areas as well as in mixed-reality solutions that incorporate aspects of both virtual and augmented reality. The gains in experience by increasing the immersiveness of our devices and allowing us to step into the data and live the data and the content are expected to be transformational in nature.

An application of these technologies that is already gaining widespread acceptance is in digital entertainment. Here videogame makers and film producers are allowing users to experience 360-degree videos where they can rotate their viewing position to see the content in 3D rather than 2D and with a 360-degree field of view. The same video game makers are also applying virtual reality to computer-generated content. The opportunity is even greater here because the content is being rendered by a computer, and the viewer can not only step into the content and view it from different directions, but can actually interact with the computer-generated assets and environments: picking up objects, physically interacting with characters, and shaping the experience. Unlike 360-degree video, which captures an image but can't then change that image, CGI VR (computer generated imagery virtual reality) allows the content to be dynamically modified as the viewer interacts with it.

An example of a very innovative company we have backed that is pushing the frontier of CGI VR in entertainment is Waygate/VRTV. Here, a team of industry veterans from Telltale Games and Zynga has created a platform that delivers fully interactive VR experiences through real-time, native 3D rendering—not video. (Note: "Native" means that the software was developed for a device and its own operating system—rather than being developed for some other operating system.) Their platform allows all of the content to be streamed in real time from the cloud directly to the user's device. This is a breakthrough when compared to the very long download times that most large VR files require, and because the content is rendered natively on each device, there is no latency, pauses, or stuttering. This means the user experience is immersive and immediate.

Of course, VR and AR are not confined to entertainment applications. We are seeing emerging companies apply these technologies across a breadth of industries: VR to help surgeons operate on patients remotely; VR that allows potential buyers in China to walk through apartments in Los Angeles and New York, admiring the views from each window, opening each door, and seeing how the surfaces will be finished; and AR applications that allow industrial equipment technicians to have instruction manuals and guides to be projected into their lines of sight as they open up industrial machinery in factories and determine how best to fix it. These are just a handful of examples from a plethora that are now being envisioned and created.

Security Software

The Internet is evolving as we continue to add increased computer power, more powerful high-speed networks, more endpoint devices, and ever-increasing amounts of content. But, the Internet is also open to less positive changes as hostile players choose to attack, for whatever purpose, the Internet and its activity. Cybersecurity and the rise of very responsive security hardware and software is the next area that investors expect to be very fruitful for new innovations. Security software also extends into the physical world. As we see the extension of new security networks into the physical world through, for example, video surveillance systems at our homes, places of work, and public places, security software needs to become ever more effective and reliable.

Viakoo is an example of another start-up we have backed that provides operational intelligence for physical security systems. Leveraging purpose-built technology, Viakoo quickly and automatically detects physical security system failures, diagnoses the problem, and then alerts users, telling them how to fix it. The company, based in Mountain View, California, is operating at the very frontier of operational intelligence in which real-time dynamic business analytics are delivering visibility and insights into data, streaming events and business operations, and, in this case, improving the integrity and effectiveness of video-based security networks.

As we will show in the next chapter, the risks inherent in cybersecurity form a potential wildcard that could interrupt the very thesis of this story: that we are entering a Fifth Era of human existence. We will return to this theme in Chapter 3, but suffice to say that the capital that will flow to security software and the arms race that is occurring in this space provide some of the rationale for why early-stage investors view this as likely to be one of the top five value-creation opportunities of our time.

FinTech and Blockchain

The financial industry has always been a highly digital industry since money has evolved over time to essentially be a digital, rather than a physical, medium in most applications in most parts of the world. Since money became digital so early, computers became essential to the financial industry and processes globally, and we saw the growth of an industry focused on technologies that support these very large industries (FinTech). Continuing breakthroughs are expected as new technologies are applied to the legacy financial infrastructure that was created at the end of the twentieth century. Foremost amongst these is the distributed ledger or blockchain, which holds the promise of allowing much more powerful real-time confirmation of trades and the people who are trading with each other. Early applications suggest that blockchain can not only improve the productivity of financial activities but also eliminate the need to maintain large, complex, and burdensome legacy infrastructure.

We are partnered with Blockchain Capital Partners, which is among the most active investors in early-stage companies that are utilizing the new innovations in the blockchain arena. We are continually impressed by how teams of entrepreneurs are finding real-world applications for blockchain both in financial services and also in other industries where transactions need to be validated in real time and where information needs to be secure and transactions recorded for future review. We are also seeing industry incumbents across industries, from banking and insurance, to healthcare and real estate, see valuable applications in their industries.

FinTech is, of course, much broader than just blockchain. Broadly defined, the financial industries, like banking, investments, insurance, trading, and so on, compose perhaps the largest industry on the face of the earth. While they were "digitized" very early, that also indicates the reality that their infrastructure is "first generation." Most large financial industry companies have aging legacy computing infrastructure that needs to be brought into the new world of cloud, big data, AI, and so on. And perhaps even more importantly, the financial industry is itself powering every other industry because it enables the workings of global commerce and transactions. We have backed two FinTech companies, ApplePie Capital and Sindeo, that focus on these convergence spaces. ApplePie Capital is a peer-to-peer lending platform that allows any franchisee to get financing while Sindeo brings a more digital-enabled platform to help real-estate investors get their financing, beginning with homebuyers.

So, FinTech is seen as a top area of future growth and wealth creation both because it is mission-critical to one of the world's largest industries and because it is enabling new transaction and payment systems to every other industry, including all of those new industries being unleashed by the Digital Revolution.

Clean Technologies

In the overview of the Industrial Era, we described the three phases through which the Industrial Era moved, powered first by coal and steam, then by other fossil fuels, and most recently by electricity. Clean technologies hold the promise that humans will be able to find even more powerful and more sustainable approaches to generating the energy sources that they need to power all of the innovations described in this section and that will come. Whether it be areas that we've explored for centuries—wind, water, and solar power—or new and emerging areas, such as fuel cells and nuclear fission and fusion, increasing investment and entrepreneurial energy is being focused on finding clean technologies for the Fifth Era. In addition, clean technologies include those innovations that help maintain the cleanliness of our air, water, and Earth for future generations.

We have made a number of investments in this space, including our support of The Clean Fund, based in California, which is the leading provider of long-term financing for energy efficiency, water conservation, renewable energy, and seismic improvements for commercial, multifamily, and other nonresidential properties in the US. For almost a decade, we have worked closely with Shanshan Group of China, the world's leading provider of lithium carbonate and a significant player in other clean energy sources. And, with Keiretsu Capital, we have invested in companies, such as Indow, which creates window inserts that reduce energy costs, Phytonix, which is an industrial biotechnology company, producing sustainable chemicals directly from carbon dioxide, and has the objective to be the global leader in biosafe, direct solar chemicals and fuel production, utilizing carbon dioxide as the sole feedstock and energy from the sun, and SafeH2O, which is a water biodetection company, providing rapid pathogen test systems and data services, assisting water providers and servicers in reducing illness, and assuring sustainability of water systems.

Clean technologies are critical to the long-term sustainable development of the earth and will be needed in the future as fossil fuels eventually become scarce and their disadvantages too burdensome. Given the almost limitless sources of energy from the sun, water and wind, most investors see future wealth generation opportunities in these areas. Additionally, investors know that a lot of money will be made cleaning up the negative impacts of Industrial Era energy sources during the time of transition to the Fifth Era.

And All the Others Too

The top seven areas of disruptive innovation detailed above show just how ubiquitous innovation will be over the next few decades as the Digital and Biotechnology Revolutions continue to transform our age.

Investors are also excited by other areas of disruptive innovation:

Continuing *advances in infrastructure applications* that enable every business to be in the cloud, connected and effective on other people's platforms, like Amazon web services, Google Enterprise and Applications, and Microsoft Azure, to name just three, is one such area.

Opportunities in the continuing *evolution of electronic commerce*, which was one of the hallmarks of the initial expansion of the Internet, allowing us to find, purchase, and receive goods and services electronically, whereas before we would have relied upon physical retailing, in most cases. The next wave of e-commerce is pushing the envelope by doing an even better job of predicting our individual needs, surfacing alternatives that are personalized to our own circumstances, and allowing us to access the products and services we want, wherever we want them, at the time that we most need them. This next phase of electronic commerce is also expected to be much more immersive, leveraging some of the breakthroughs we've already described in areas, such as big data analytics and AI, in VR and AR, relying upon the breakthroughs of the blockchain and financial technologies, and potentially also incorporating IoT and wearables breakthroughs. This compounding of innovations is a theme that is important and one that we'll return to later.

We continue to see more and more powerful *endpoint devices* as described already. As social animals, it's no surprise that one of the major uses to which we apply this real-time connected capability is to communicate with other human beings. New breakthroughs in social media are allowing us to do that in more and more rich and robust ways. And, we still need to connect another one or two billion people into that conversation.

In the past, we've entertained ourselves through a variety of media, including books, newspapers, films, radio, TV, music, and so on. Most of these entertainment formats are broadcast formats. Conversely, nowadays most people seek to interact during their entertainment, and many people want to be a part of creating the entertainment experience. People's desire for more interactivity and the ability to express their own creativity is something that new technologies are beginning to enable at an ever-increasing rate. *Immersive, interactive entertainment* holds the promise that we will all become creators of entertainment experiences and fully immersed in the experiences that we create with others.

In the travel industry, we see two dimensions of rapid expansion and growth. The first is that a greater percentage of the population of the world is beginning to travel, and we're seeing hundreds of millions of people, including in China and India, getting to a level of affluence where travel for entertainment is an option for them. Secondly, we're also seeing the expansion of virtual travel where people use some of the technologies we've already described to have virtual travel experiences, enabling them to go places where, in practice, they would never be able to travel physically. This part of the *digital travel experience* is expected both to be a very substantial growth opportunity and also a potential disruptor of traditional modes of tourism and travel.

We have been placing our own bets in all of these areas too—Acceleration Systems and Curb in infrastructure applications, 1World Online, Perkville, and Social Standards in ecommerce and social, Telltale Games, Soundwave, and Spotify in digital entertainment, and LesConcierges/John Paul in the new travel industry—just to mention a handful.

Do These Innovations Make a Positive Difference?

Disruptive innovations bring with them disruption and change—by definition. In most cases, an established business or activity is disrupted while a new business or activity is created. At this point in our story, it makes sense to ask: Is this, on balance, positive for the world and for humankind? On balance, do disruptive innovations, like we are seeing today, move us forward? Do they create more than they destroy?

The answer is—yes they do, when viewed from an economic perspective. A recent study by researchers from our alma mater, Stanford University, confirms this. Researchers Kogan, Papanikolaou, Seru and Stoffman (2016) just completed an analysis of all patents issued to US firms between 1926 and 2010. They assessed the degree to which these patents created scientific and economic value and creative destruction.

Across all three metrics they were able to show high levels of positive gain associated with the patent activity. From an economic perspective, disruptive innovations make a positive difference.

Societally, are these disruptive innovations also positive? This is a harder question to answer because it requires us to know what the future of society will look like and then make a personal judgment as to whether we value that future higher than the current society(ies) in which we live today. We don't have the answer to this second question. For us, we believe that the value that disruptive innovations bring by solving society's most pressing problems has never been greater— whether we are talking about the need for clean air, water, and earth, more food for everyone, better healthcare and longer life, improved working conditions, more availability of knowledge and education, sustainable sources of clean energy, less congestion in our cities, and so forth. We are sure that the technologies and approaches that got 7.5 billion of us to this point will not be able to solve the challenging issues of today, let alone those that will surface in the future. Only new innovations will make sure that our children, and their children, live in a world where these and many other issues have been solved.

Never has it been so true that necessity must be the mother of invention—the greatest challenges of our time demand innovative solutions.

By now, you have reviewed examples of the types of disruptive innovations that are coming, or perhaps you have your own view—and as Mahatma Gandhi said, "You must be the change you wish to see in the world."

A World of Opportunities Ahead

To conclude this chapter, the world is seeing incredible opportunities being created by a breadth of disruptive innovations. And, there is much more coming. We don't know what the list of top innovations will be when a future survey is taken in 2117. What we do know is that it will be profoundly shaped by the Digital Revolution, the Biotechnology Revolution, and the compounding of the two. We also know that many of the long list of disruptive innovations that inventors are currently working on and that we have just described will have been deployed globally and across industries, transforming our lives and improving the condition of humankind.

Gordon Moore, co-founder of Intel, the world's leading semi-conductor company, observed in 1965 that "the number of transistors per square inch on integrated circuits has doubled every year since the integrated circuit was invented." He went on to predict that this trend would continue for the foreseeable future. We know this as Moore's law.

If we, Matthew Le Merle and Alison Davis, were to seek to create a similar law for the Fifth Era, it would be that "the compounding of digital with biotechnology innovations will accelerate disruptive change at a rate that humankind has never experienced before. We can only begin to imagine just how different the Fifth Era will be."

Because these innovations are so very different from the incremental changes that occurred within the phases of the Industrial Era, we feel absolutely confident that they, in total, represent the shift to a new era—and that we are living in a time of transition.

In the next chapter, we will explore just how different living in the Fifth Era might be.

Chapter 3
Glimpses of the Fifth Era

Change is the law of life. And those who look only to the past or present are certain to miss the future.

—John F. Kennedy

Another lens through which to view this Fifth Era is to explore specific aspects of human beings and see if these innovations would change us dramatically or not. If not, then perhaps we are just evolving the Industrial Era into a new phase. If it is likely that how we behave and interact as human beings is likely to change dramatically, then we are certainly in a new era.

Let's explore how different the future might be and the magnitude of the disruption and wealth creation that is likely to occur.

Human Activities Built upon Underlying Assumptions

In each era, humans conduct their activities within the modus operandi of the era. They live and work and play within an "era mindset," a set of underlying assumptions, methods, and beliefs that is so established that it shapes their view as to what is possible and, as a result, what can be. But, when disruptive innovations attack that mindset and those underlying assumptions, we tend to see inertia continue the old ways of being longer than is strictly necessary. It takes a while for disruptive innovations to enable new ways of being and for the old order to be displaced. This is why transitions between eras are not clean and linear, but rather messy, overlapping, and chaotic, and it is only when old ways of being have been displaced that we move into the next era.

Let's look at three central aspects of our lives in the Industrial Era and see if they are still likely to be the way that they have been. Are the underlying assumptions on which they were designed still valid? Or, have disruptive innovations knocked out the Industrial Era rationale for their design, providing the preconditions for new approaches?

Generation C

In order to examine areas of our lives, we should first introduce the notion of Generation C (see Sidebar 2). This is the portion of the world's population that was born after 1990 and has only known a connected existence. They are unaware of a time before the Internet and don't understand many of the assumptions that shape the mindsets of older people and rule their decisions and actions. Yes, we have heard of Generations X, Y, and Z, but we see them all as vertical slices through a more fundamental transition—from our generation, generally born before 1990, and which grew up in an unconnected world—to a new generation, Generation C, that is growing up always connected into the whole.

In 2010, we were part of a team at Booz & Company, the consulting firm (now a part of PWC) that surveyed this "connected generation" around the world. We found that this Generation C simply does not think in the same way as prior generations. They are ready for new approaches that the next era is ready to unleash.

Sidebar 2: Generation C

By the year 2020, an entire generation will have grown up in a primarily digital world. Computers, the Internet, mobile phones, texting, social networking—all are second nature to them. And their familiarity with technology, reliance on mobile communications, and desire to remain in contact with large networks of family members, friends, business contacts, and others will transform how we work and how we consume. This is the demographic group we call Generation C—the C stands for connect, communicate, change.

What Is Generation C?

What is Generation C? They are realists, they are materialists. They are culturally liberal, if not politically progressive. They are upwardly mobile, yet they live with their parents longer than others ever did. Many of their social interactions take place on the Internet, where they feel free to express their opinions and attitudes. They've grown up under the influence of Harry Potter, Barack Obama, and iEverything—iPods, iTunes, iPhones. Technology is so intimately woven into their lives that the concept of "early adopter" is essentially meaningless.

They are Generation C—connected, communicating, content-centric, computerized, community-oriented, always clicking. As a rule, they were born after 1990 and lived their adolescent years after 2000. In the developed world, Generation C encompasses everyone in this age group; in the BRIC countries, they are primarily urban and suburban. By 2020, they will make up 40 percent of the population in the US, Europe, and the BRIC countries, and 10 percent in the rest of the world—and by then, they will constitute the largest group of consumers worldwide.

Having owned digital devices all their lives, they are intimately familiar with them and use them as much as six hours a day. They all have mobile phones and constantly send text messages. More than 95 percent of them have computers, and more than half use instant messaging to communicate, have Facebook pages, and watch videos on YouTube.

Consider the typical Gen C "digital native" in 2020—Colin is a 20-year-old computer science student in London, where he lives with two other students on the equivalent of about €600 a month. He enjoys backpacking, sports, music, and gaming. He has a primary digital device (PDD) that keeps him connected 24 hours a day—at home, in transit, and at school.

He uses it to download and record music, video, and other content, and to keep in touch with his family, friends, and an ever-widening circle of acquaintances. His apartment is equipped with the latest wireless home technology with download speeds mandated by the government.

Colin's parents are divorced, and he has one sister. He is close to his family, but his actual physical contact with them is limited. Instead, he prefers to stay in touch through his PDD, which allows him to communicate simultaneously through multiple channels—voice, text, video, data—either to them individually or to all of them at once. His parents would prefer that he visit more often, of course, but they are finally beginning to get used to being a part of his digital life. Still, sometimes Colin feels he is too digitally connected; for example, a recent surprise visit to his mother was ruined because she knew he was in town—he had forgotten to disable the location feature on his PDD. Colin's social life is also mediated through his PDD. He can always find out the location of his friends, even what they are doing, and communicate with them instantly.

Much of Colin's experience at school is mediated by his PDD. He can attend lectures, browse reading material, do research, compare notes with classmates, and even take exams—all from the comfort of his apartment. When he does go to campus, his PDD automatically connects to the school's network and downloads relevant content, notices, even bills for fees, and he can authorize their payment later, at his leisure. His PDD does most of the work for him when he's shopping too. Though he prefers to shop online, when he does visit a store, the PDD automatically connects to the store's network, guiding him through product choices, offering peer reviews, and automatically checking out and paying for items he purchases.

Colin's real passion is traveling, preferably with backpack. On a recent trip to Australia, his PDD kept him occupied throughout the long plane ride, then helped him through customs by automatically connecting to the Australian government's network. Colin used the PDD to pinpoint the location of Australian friends he was going to travel with (he had met them on the Internet). Once they met up, they used their PDDs to plan their route, a relatively easy task, given that with the entire world was already modeled in 3D they could see every twist and turn on their path. No surprises there!

Exhibit 12
A Day in the Life of a Generation C Consumer, 2020

20-Year Old Leo Q's Day: April 12, 2020

7:00 Reading news on personal digital device (PDD)
– Twittering plans for the day

7:30 Checking e-health tool: first symptoms of sinusitis; message on PDD for doctor's appointment

8:00 E-vote on "ban of motor vehicles in Berlin governmental area" referendum via "digital ID"

9:00 Interactive video e-learning session with professor

11:30 Short video chat with grandmother - Sharing tasks via cloud project tool

13:30 Navigation-supported drive to doctor
– Real-time smart routing to avoid traffic congestion

15:30 Unlock clinical record for doctor; medication sent to home

18:00 Shopping downtown: online price check with PDD, friend recommendations on intended couch purchase
– Shopping tour picture sharing on profile

19:30 Downtown walk: friends join for location-based 30% discount promotion for dinner at small restaurant
– M-payment for food

22:30 Retiring: e-book and simultaneous streamed video
– Automated reminder via PDD to take sinusitis medication before 23:00

Sources: Fredrich R., Le Merle M., Peterson M., Koster A. (2010)

We will now look at aspects of how we make friends, how we learn, and how we work, as three examples to make the general case that all human activities are being impacted by the innovations that surround us today.

How We Make Friends

Making friends is one of the most important human activities in that it is a foundation for all social endeavors.

How Many Friends Do You Have?

We asked members of our generation and members of Generation C a handful of questions. First, we asked, "How many friends do you have?" Members of our generation, generally born before 1990, typically say 100, more or less. Generation C typically says more—maybe 250 or 300.

How Many Have You Met?

We then asked both groups, "How many of your friends have you met in person?" Our generation laughs, replying, "All of them, of course." Generation C responds with a perfectly straight face, "Most of them I haven't met." They don't see this as an odd question at all. Why do you need to physically meet people to be friends with them? "What a strange concept," they seem to say.

How Do You Define a Friend?

Then we asked both groups, "What makes a friend a friend?" Both generations answer very similarly: a friend is someone you know, trust, share confidences with in both directions, use as a sounding board, appreciate having the support of, etc. Both our generation and Generation C have the same definition of what a friend is.

What Do You Do With Your Friends?

Next we explored with both groups what they do with their friends. How often do they interact? When was the last interaction? What confidences have they shared recently? What confidences have their friends shared? And so on.

And we find, consistently, that Generation C is living up to the definition of friendship with their friends while our generation is not. Indeed, by the very definition of friendship given by those in our generation, our generation has even fewer friends than they declared at the outset while in many cases Generation C has more.

Whose Friends Are More Real?

So, who has more friends and whose friends are more real? The answer is Generation C. Why? Because they have released themselves from the Industrial Era mindset that friendships need to be physically based and because they have embraced digital innovations that allow them to build virtual friendships with people they have not yet met in person.

Why is this such a dramatic example? Because, if society can build deep and enduring, trust-based relationships so easily with people that have never been met in person and if those friendships can be made to endure and can be multiplied and maintained in ever-larger numbers, this in turn greatly expands the scope and scale of so many other human activities in connected, real-time, and continuous ways. This impacts learning, socializing, entertaining, working, and every other human activity.

How We Learn

Let's consider a second part of our lives that has similarly been transformed by the Digital Revolution. Learning is the work of a lifetime, and humans learn all the time. However, to illustrate the most important themes of this chapter, let's focus on one particular component of learning—higher education and the role of universities and colleges of higher learning. We've made this the focus because it is the pinnacle of our organized learning process today. We can expect insights we derive from this focus to ripple back down into the school system towards our earliest days, as well as forward into corporate and continuing learning systems.

The University in the Industrial Era

The university, including colleges of higher education, is a globally accepted element of how we are educated within the Industrial Era. While some early universities began to appear in the Agrarian Era and many more were formed in the Mercantile Era, the university became universally accepted as the principal approach to higher education during the Industrial Era, displacing private tutoring, the apprentice system, and self-learning.

In the fall of 2016, some 20.5 million students were in attendance at American colleges and universities, constituting an increase of about 5.2 million since fall 2000. About 7.2 million students will attend two-year institutions, and 13.3 million will attend four-year institutions.

Some 17.5 million students enrolled in undergraduate programs, and about 3.0 million enrolled in post-baccalaureate programs (National Center for Education Statistics, 2016).

Why?

University: The Underlying Assumptions

During the Agrarian Era, knowledge was in short supply. Those who had it were rare. Most people did not read or write, and most people were not formally educated. A few people were exceptions to that rule. They sought out knowledge, wrote it down—by hand—and were willing to share it with like-minded people.

Because they were so few, they clustered together, around libraries that hosted the carefully hand-written scrolls and early books that documented their knowledge, or they met around a tree, in a courtyard, or in a chamber and talked to each other.

If you wanted to learn, you had no choice but to travel to these few locations. Most people were not wealthy enough to be able to afford the trip or the time off from farming the land. Those few that did, arrived in the place of knowledge, and listened and learned. Perhaps they stayed or perhaps they returned home.

After the invention of the printing press, more knowledge could be captured and shared, but even then the learned teachers were few in number. And they still preferred to cluster. They remained in centers of knowledge and agreed to teach in those places.

Over time these locations became more established, more formalized, more populated. And the role of teacher and student became more accepted and established.

Over time the university was born.

The University: Disrupting the Underlying Assumptions

Now let's look again at each of those underlying assumptions through the most recent lens of this time of transition. As we look, we'll pose the question, "Is this underlying assumption still true?"

Knowledge is in short supply—is this assumption still true? No. Today most knowledge is captured and instantly available to anyone anywhere. This is one of the great benefits of the Internet and those who have made the world's knowledge available to everyone.

Those who have this knowledge are rare—is this assumption still true? No. Today indexes and searches allow anyone to explore the available knowledge and find what they are seeking. Additionally, most knowledge has been captured and stored online.

Most people do not read or write—is this assumption still true? No. Over the last part of the Industrial Era almost everyone around the world has become literate: the World Factbook estimates 82% of the world's population is now in this group (Central Intelligence Agency, 2016).

Knowledge has to be concentrated into libraries—is this assumption still true? No. Knowledge can be everywhere in the cloud and accessible everywhere through the Internet.

People need to meet physically to learn—is this assumption still true? Maybe. While remote electronic learning can be effective, especially for the connected generation that views this as their preferred learning mode (see Sidebar 2: Generation C), for many, and especially for the teachers who were brought up in the old model, physical teaching and tutoring still has its merits.

Most people are not wealthy enough to attend university—is this assumption still true? No. Once the costs of the physical university and attending it in person are removed from the equation, the cost of accessing the knowledge, having it taught, and learning it becomes trivial. It is the physical model of the university, with the need for un-leveraged teachers and expensive buildings and grounds, that drives the cost of that model.

In short, the Digital Revolution has undermined every underlying assumption for why we have universities as centers of learning. Of course, exceptions still exist. For example, certain laboratory or research activities still need to be performed in physical locations. Even here we are creating virtual simulations that may undermine these exceptions.

So, why do we still have universities?

Because teachers and parents were themselves taught in the

Industrial Era model and have not become comfortable with the Fifth Era innovations and because of inertia and the sizable legacy infrastructure of buildings, classrooms, libraries, residence halls, athletic facilities, and so on.

Does this inertia mean that we will never see virtual learning of high education knowledge?

We don't think so. The disruptive innovations of the Digital Revolution have already enabled a transition of higher education from the Industrial Era model to a new Fifth Era model of virtual learning. But, it will take time for new ways to displace old ways. Maybe decades, maybe centuries. Maybe faster. Notwithstanding this uncertainty over the transition timing, there is sure to be a significant wealth-creation opportunity for those who lead in the creation and deployment of the new Fifth Era learning models.

How Fast Could This Change?

In parts of the world where physical institutions of higher learning have already been built, there is more resistance to changing the underlying model. In parts of the world where physical institutions of higher learning have not been built, the case for change gets more notice and support.

Consider China. China's population was more than 1.35 billion in 2016. An increasing proportion of the Chinese population is "middle class" and expect access to good education for their children. By 2022 McKinsey and Company expects 75% of Chinese to be middle class (Barton, Chen, & Jin, 2013). With a large and growing inland Chinese middle class (McKinsey estimates they will represent 39% of the total Chinese middle class by 2022) located in the inland cities where there is limited access to the best learning, what should the Chinese do? Build vast numbers of physical universities across the country? Allow their students to travel to the coastal cities? Ship them to American universities? Perhaps, all of the above?

Given the disruptive innovations of recent years, why not promote virtual learning and allow students to remain where they are, join virtual classrooms, and get educated according to a new model? This is the thrust of the very significant rise in remote technology-enabled learning across China. We have recently joint ventured with Talkweb, one of China's leading technology-enabled learning platforms and their growth is quite remarkable.

Who Will Capture the Opportunity?

Who will win? Again, it is not clear. A priori there is value in the existing university brands and teaching excellence. If branded institutions, like our alma maters Cambridge, Harvard, Oxford, and Stanford, embrace the new world and work hard to solve the remaining challenges, then surely they have an advantage since they have brands, reputations, and a great number of other assets developed over hundreds of years and not shared by start-ups. Why would upstarts and start-ups be better positioned?

Why do we highlight higher education and learning? Because, if we can move to approaches in which all of the world's 7.5 billion people (and one day many more) can gain the full benefits of human knowledge through scalable, inexpensive, and universally available learning platforms, then surely we have an opportunity to unleash the full capability of so many more billions of people than we are able to today.

Imagine what humankind could achieve if 10 or 100 or 1,000 times as many people were able to bring their full potentials to bear on our most pressing issues through the power of virtual learning, collaboration, and problem-solving platforms.

How We Work

Here is one last example to illustrate our thesis: that the Industrial Era's underlying assumptions have been undermined by new disruptive technologies, which, in turn, are opening up enormous new opportunities for entrepreneurs and the people that back them.

Work - Our Invention

Work is the greatest invention of the Industrial Era. In the Hunter-Gatherer Era it was not even a notion. You did what you needed to do to sustain yourself, and the rest of your time was for you. But, in the

Industrial Era the rise of the corporate model of business and everything that went with it established almost universal beliefs and expectations about "work," assumptions that we live with today, that rule our lives and shape many of our notions of what a life even looks like.

How Does Our Generation Define Work?

When asked, our generation (people generally born before 1990) defers to a definition of work that is the result of how things were done in the Industrial Era. We talk about work needing a workplace. Work is something that has defined hours—typically Monday to Friday from 9 am until 5 pm. There are employers who are mostly large corporations, and there are bosses in a hierarchical pyramid who direct our work and whom we report to. We expect to work in the same job for many years—sometimes for a lifetime. And when we eventually retire, we expect to be supported either by the companies we worked a lifetime for or by government-created support programs funded by those companies and by taxes.

How Does Generation C Define It?

Then ask Generation C how they define work. They have very different answers. Work is something you do to make the money to pursue your other interests. It is something you do when you want to. Sometimes you may have one employer, sometimes you have several, and sometimes you do work on your own. You expect not only to have many jobs over your lifetime, but also at any given time. It is not "moonlighting," it is your choice to do as many jobs as you want. Maybe you take time off from one job to do another. Maybe you do a second job at lunchtime or on your computer during downtime in your first job. Employers, bosses, defined hours, and defined places of work are notions recognized by Generation C, but the logic for them is often not understood. "Why should we go to an office if we can do work more effectively remotely?" "We get much more done on our computer, so why do our older work colleagues insist on burning up most of the day in conference room meetings?" "Let's just agree on the work that needs doing on a shared online document and get it done." "I am at my best when I do what I need to do in the order that makes sense to me." "I don't understand why others prescribe my work style to me when they don't understand how my generation and I work?"

Who Is right?

Of course, both are right. Because they are each adhering to the respective beliefs of their times. But, Generation C is right for the future. Because the future is theirs and work will change to fit the preferences and expectations of the future generation, we should expect that they will change the working approaches and practices that no longer make sense in a digitally enabled world. But, the transition time may be long. Concepts, like "the sharing economy," "services on-demand," "virtual workplaces," and so on, are fundamentally important because they are the first experiments in creating new working practices that better fit people's future new realities. While any one of these experiments may fail, they are still evidence of a growing gap between how we work in the final stages of the Industrial Era and how we will work in the Fifth Era. They are glimpses into the future of work and the workplace.

Breaking from Assumptions Creates Opportunities

By now, some readers may be saying to themselves that we, the authors of this book, don't understand the importance of physical interactions and in-person relationships, and that we are wrong and overstating the prospects of the virtual. Perhaps that is true to some extent. But do be open to challenging your own mindset. What underlying assumptions are you believing? What assumptions are you finding hard to let go? What makes these underlying assumptions "unbreakable" for you? Are the stories you tell yourself really true? Are you sure that Generation C will believe in those assumptions and will share your mindset?

At this juncture let us state an important belief: the people who best capture the opportunity of new and disruptive innovations are those who are best able to disengage from the underlying assumptions of the past, imagine how human activity can be disrupted in the future, and then build the new approaches and companies to bring those to the world.

Disruptive innovators are very good at letting go of the mindsets of the past. They are very good at breaking from assumptions that most of us hold as inviolable.

Take a look at one example of a disrupter who has made a fortune by unlocking a new business model that resulted from his refusal to accept conventional wisdom: Adam Neuman, who founded WeWork in 2010 in New York, recently visited California to discuss further expansion of the company.

To understand WeWork, first let's consider the world of office space. In the world of office space, most people have no choice but to sign multi-year leases on small office spaces, frequently in isolated corridors in large office buildings. In the past, when we accumulated a lot of equipment, filing cabinets, and bookcases, and did most of our work at desks and on the office telephone, a physical office space was typically necessary. This was true both for small firms and new companies starting out.

Adam noticed that the arrival of the digital economy had created a number of new realities that were challenging this old model of office work. For example, today most of us keep most of our information virtually and don't need files, bookcases, and so forth. We transact our business more often than not electronically on mobile devices, not fixed landlines. We don't need large conference rooms, reception areas, and receptionists very often anymore. We just don't need to "own" all of that space all of the time.

Meanwhile, the costs of forming new businesses have fallen, and the next generation of entrepreneurs is more comfortable creating new businesses in serial fashion, starting one after another until something gets traction. They can't be sure how long one entrepreneurial venture will last, so it does not make sense to make long-term commitments for potentially short-lived ventures.

Why should they have to sign a multi-year lease on a space larger than they need? And why should they have to hire dedicated support personnel when the office landlord can provide those people and spread them in support of a host of tenants, thus gaining cost synergies in the process?

Adam saw that the dominant form of office space in the city was ripe for disruption—at least on behalf of a new generation of young entrepreneurial tenants, even if big companies preferred to maintain the multi-year lease model.

So, WeWork was launched as a new flexible office format with pay-as-you-go arrangements and services available on demand. Any individual or company can base itself at a WeWork office location taking as small an amount of space as they need—from a private office, to a dedicated desk, to a "hot desk" shared with others on a first-come, first-served basis each day. This space is taken on a monthly basis, so multi-year contracts are not required. Meanwhile, WeWork provides additional services, such as:

- Super fast Internet
- Access to business printers
- Onsite business support staff
- Free refreshments
- Networking events
- Meetings with experts and investors

Today WeWork has dozens of locations on several continents and a valuation in excess of $16 billion. WeWork is only seven years old as we write. Many believe that flexible workspace is the future and in only a few decades it will replace the old model around the world—at least for those tenants that prefer this new model.

Characteristics of the Fifth Era

These examples, in which long-held human activities built upon underlying assumptions are now being rethought because of the disruptive innovations of our time, are only a few of many. Indeed, every aspect of human existence is being impacted. Some years ago we co-authored a paper on "The Next Wave of Digitization" intended for corporate executives. In it we summarized the three driving forces that are making this digitization phenomenon possible. The summary of this paper is included as Sidebar 3: Three Driving Forces.

Sidebar 3: Three Driving Forces

The outlines of the fully digitized world have long been sketched. So, why are we reaching this critical inflection point now? The reason is that three driving forces, acting in concert, are powerfully reinforcing one another.

Consumer Pull

Consumers, and particularly Generation C, are already fully adapted to the digital environment. They expect to be connected every moment of their lives, through virtually every device, whether they are consuming news and entertainment, reaching out to their friends through social media, such as Facebook and Twitter, or mixing work with play as they go through the working day. Their insistence on the right to stay connected is transforming their personal lives, and their willingness to share everything is changing long-held attitudes about privacy. Their trust is shifting from well-known brands to referrals from their closest friends. They are advocates of many causes and at the same time deeply embedded in their social environments. In their world, knowledge isn't just power. It's social and commercial currency—and access to it is vital. These changes are forcing companies to rethink how to manage their employees, who are already becoming less emotionally attached to their company's wider purpose and goals and who expect to be able to live their digital lives at work as well as at home. These trends are spreading outward from the developed world, as new middle-class populations in every emerging market are being connected to the global information flow. The typical Generation C consumer now spends a large portion of their day online, always connected, always communicating.

Technology Push

Digital technology continues to make inroads into every aspect of our lives. The infrastructure backbone of the digital world is expanding into every corner of the globe, bringing affordable wired and wireless broadband to billions of consumers in developed and developing markets alike. Three-quarters of the world's population is now connected through mobile phones while digital cloud-based services gather more and more data on consumers in every segment. In parallel with the "Internet of People," low-cost connected sensors and devices are being deployed in every industry. The development of cloud computing, and the vast information processing machinery it requires, is well under way. As a result, the demand for powerful real-time analytics engines to allow companies to gather and make sense of hitherto "undigested" information flows is rising fast, and companies around the world are responding with new technologies, such as in-memory analytics devices, to meet that need.

Economic Benefits

The third force driving the digitization phenomenon is the realization on the part of executives in every industry that the economic benefits to be captured are real. Though it is too early to quantify those benefits, a wave of capital has poured into the new digitization technologies and companies, and the public markets are beginning to reward early movers with valuations reminiscent of the years leading up to the dot-com bubble. An increasing portion of the $22 billion and the $20 billion that US venture capital firms and US angel investors, respectively, invest each year appears to be going into these digitization technologies. Recent transactions in the secondary financial markets have suggested that Facebook is worth more than $80 billion while LinkedIn recently went public at a valuation of more than $3.3 billion, a high multiple over its 2010 revenues of $243 million. On a national scale, the benefits of digitization created through investments in broadband infrastructure have been amply demonstrated.

Meanwhile, the economic cycle and globalization have exposed the weaknesses of large enterprises that have so far failed to embrace digitization. They have also sharpened the minds of CEOs regarding the need to further cut costs and monetize existing capabilities more effectively. Finally, increased competition from around the world is forcing companies in every industry to contend with increased cost pressures, transforming their traditional value chains, spawning new formats and new business models, blurring industry boundaries, and even creating entire new industries. In response, companies are turning to digitization to provide a competitive advantage and to generate growth.

At the sovereign level, too, countries and regions are acting to accelerate the digitization phenomenon. China has written cloud, connectivity, and digitization goals into its twelfth five-year plan, which will include

> stimulus measures estimated at more than $1.7 trillion. The European Union has agreed on an energy upgrade plan of more than $200 billion, and the UK's national infrastructure plan earmarks more than $200 billion.
>
> Source: Friedrich, R., Le Merle, M., Peterson, M., & Koster, A. (2011). The next wave of digitization—Setting your direction, building your capabilities. Booz & Company.

The purpose of this chapter is not to detail all of the characteristics of the Fifth Era, but we would like to share our list of the top fifteen characteristics of the Fifth Era that we see as particularly important to watch and track. They are:

Top 15 Characteristics of the Fifth Era

1. The development of an entirely digital world in which information, communication, and collaboration are comprehensive and instantaneous.

2. The invention of new and unimaginable innovations at the intersection of the Digital Revolution and the Biotechnology Revolution and a constant flow of a host of other disruptive innovations feeding off the global availability of knowledge and new collaborative innovation approaches.

3. Addressable target markets rapidly becoming global, allowing disruptive innovations to quickly be adopted by billions of people (assuming our "Wildcard 1: Balkanization of the Global Economic System" does not get played—see below).

4. Consumers gaining enormously as the choices they have will be multiplied by a host of competing solutions and providers, and prices will fall given the economies of scale provided by serving global markets.

5. There will be a reevaluation of what humans value and what makes us happy, with significant implications for markets for consumer goods and services. The next generations may value simplicity/less over clutter/excess and experiences over material goods.

6. A dramatic increase in productivity. But, this time it will not just be increases in labor productivity. Instead, physical asset productivity will also be greatly enhanced, and formerly unproductive assets will be made available for others to use on demand.

7. The Industrial Era large corporate model of organization will be challenged, with the largest companies increasingly extending their enterprises beyond their four walls and looking more like virtual entities.

8. Public markets will need to evolve to address their shortcomings, for example short-termism.

9. Private capital will drive the initial stages of development for most emerging innovations capturing much of the value of new disruptive innovations.

10. Sustainability will become an essential part of doing business with a clear focus on the broader societal impacts of company strategies including the quality of jobs, the full impact of products and services on society and other external considerations.

11. People will have much more freedom to spend their time according to their desires. Multi-tasking, parallel working, and short-lived organizations and workgroups will be the norm, and the very notion of work will change.

12. Distributed innovation will be everywhere, with no monopoly on innovation by any one company, country, or region. Most innovation will come from small, emerging players, with large corporations being the "go-to-market" partners for innovators.

13. There will be a global war for talent as every digital innovation hub and every region and country try to keep their own technology innovators home and attract those of neighboring regions in order to further strengthen their innovation economies.

14. The power of diversity will be increasingly understood and leveraged.

15. Traditional philanthropy and the for-profit model will come closer together as non-profits look at becoming more sustainable in social entrepreneurship models, and as for-profit corporations aim for double and triple bottom line outcomes.

Because of these changes, every industry, every profit pool, in every country, will be fundamentally challenged as we move into the Fifth Era. We believe that it is possible to already see significant new areas of economic opportunity and wealth creation by divining carefully through these glimpses of the future and making a few bets.

At this point, we expect that many of our readers will be asking, "Why aren't the authors naming the new era? If the second era was called the Agrarian, and the fourth the Industrial, what should be the name of the Fifth Era?" For our part, we think it is too early to say. We know some of the outlines of the future, and we are sure it will be very different from today and driven by the disruptive innovations that we are experiencing today and expect to surface tomorrow—impelled by the twin forces of the Digital and Biotechnology Revolutions. But, there are a lot of plausible futures for how the Fifth Era manifests. We recommend that we simply call it the "Fifth Era" for another twenty or thirty years by which time we expect that the essence of this future era will be coming into clearer focus.

Is the Fifth Era Guaranteed?

At this point in the book, we need to cover our bases. So far, we have driven down one road as quickly as possible, a road we contend is almost certainly going to prove to be the one that society takes over the next few decades. This is the road to the Fifth Era.

But, is it definitely the road to the future? Are there no turnings from it? Is it assured that society will reach this new destination?

We see a few ways in which society could step off the road or at least take a turn that might end up being a dead end or take the long way around to the same destination. We call these "wildcards." Let's share three with you, each of which keeps us up at night because they might just block the road to the Fifth Era.

- Wildcard 1: Balkanization of the Global Economic System
- Wildcard 2: Cybersecurity Crises and Failures
- Wildcard 3: Regulation and Anti-Technology Protectionism

We will briefly review each in turn.

Wildcard 1: Balkanization of the Global Economic System

The Internet is a global phenomenon. It was greatly accelerated by a time of globalization in which most countries in the world agreed to share content, encourage cross-border trade and commerce, and where most people were willing to collaborate with most other people. Holdouts exist of course: the great firewall of China, North Korea's "Kwangmyong" or "Bright" Internet cut off from the rest of the world and hosted in China with perhaps a handful of websites compared to the hundreds of millions on the world's Internet. But, these are the exceptions. Most of the world's 190-plus countries are open to the global Internet and participate more or less in the global economic system.

What would happen to the Fifth Era if this were not true? What if the world went instead in the direction of George Orwell's novel *1984* that features, among other things, three perpetually warring totalitarian super-states that choose not to cooperate with each other?

In George Orwell's novel there are three "balkanized" super-states:

- **Oceania** (Western Hemisphere, the British Isles, Australasia, and Southern Africa)

- **Eurasia** (Continental Europe and Russia, including Siberia)

- **Eastasia** (China, Japan, Korea, and Indochina)

In *1984*, these three states wage a perpetual war in "the disputed area," which is an area encompassing Northern Africa, the Middle East, India, and Indonesia. This is a place of war, slave labor, and constant chaos.

Perhaps, we don't need to go quite that far.

What if the USA/Europe, China and satellites, and Russia and satellites, for example, simply decided to erect firewalls and operate their own Internets behind those firewalls? Three Internets instead of one? With three disconnected bodies of content and separate worlds of commerce and interaction?

And, what if that went a little further? Perhaps, the physical flow of goods and services would be greatly reduced, embargoes, quotas, and tariffs more widespread, and travel, migration (immigration and emigration), and interaction more controlled and limited.

Over time, perhaps, innovation breakthroughs would not be shared, knowledge would not flow, and the world would diverge.

Would we eventually reach the Fifth Era—a globally-connected and collaborating world? Or, would we stop short in a balkanized world?

Would there be less opportunity? Or, would there be three zones of rather smaller opportunity—but more in total?

As we write this in 2017, George Orwell's writings do not seem to be completely lacking in predictive merit.

Wildcard 2: Cybersecurity Crises and Failures

The Internet has transformed every aspect of our content sharing, communications, commerce, and entertainment globally. Today every industry relies upon aspects of the digital economy to conduct their business activities and to connect to other entities: vendors, sales and marketing partners, customers, service vendors, and so on. In addition, new products and services are being built with innovations of the Digital Revolution built into them. Products that rely on the cloud, global positioning systems, cyber authorization, validation and transactional systems, and more are now the norm.

Crime has always been a part of human activity, and bad actors and bad practices have always entered the picture whenever large economic gains can be made through illegally attacking legitimate activities. However, just as the Digital Revolution has made legitimate commerce much more easy to effect on a global scale, so the Digital Revolution has also enabled the bad actors. It has also created a host of powerful new weapons for sovereign state actors to use, both in peacetime spying and in states of war, the latter, of course, being the ultimate "wildcard." Mankind could destroy its own ability to operate in a digitally connected way should state actors in time of war destroy the viability of the digital infrastructure upon which a future era depends.

Meanwhile, private bad actors come in all shapes and sizes. There are those who are principally out for economic gain and may conduct identity theft, scams of all sorts in which they trick others into paying them, fraudulent transactions for commercial activities to their benefit, and so on. There are also bad actors who philosophically disagree with the activities of others—be they at the individual, group, or societal levels. These actors are perhaps more threatening in that they may seek to disrupt new era activities without any need for the underlying digital systems to continue operating after they have completed their bad acts (in marked contrast to the economically motivated bad actors who need the Internet to operate just as much as anyone else). These disruptors are of greatest threat to the viability of a society that has become dependent upon cyber systems. The unprecedented scale of new technology-enabled criminals has taken authorities by surprise, and in many cases, those that seek to police legitimate activity have been lagging those who seek to criminally take advantage. Viruses, malicious code, identify theft on a massive scale, and so on are everyday newspaper headlines today.

In every part of the world, governments are beginning to establish institutions to address this rising tide of cybercrime, and private entities, with their products and services, are also becoming more widespread as money can be made in protecting vulnerable players.

We view this as a wildcard because we are not convinced this battle can be won. Time will tell.

Wildcard 3: Regulation and Anti-Technology Protectionism

The digital economy is driving innovation and growth around the world. As new technologies, business models, and companies are emerging, they are fundamentally altering the business landscape and the ways that traditional industries operate. While this is driving GDP and job growth in most countries, it also provides new challenges to lawmakers. The regulatory landscape has been evolving rapidly as the Internet continues to expand into all areas of business and personal life, and as lawmakers respond to the issues and concerns that are brought to them. While new regulations can potentially boost growth, they also raise the real risk of negatively impacting the investment environment and the success of Internet companies and the growth they represent. Lawmakers are considering new regulations in areas, including 1) copyright and intellectual property, 2) intermediary liability protection and censorship, 3) privacy and security, and 4) mobile infrastructure and services.

In order to ensure that the views of Internet investors are incorporated into the thinking of lawmakers, Fifth Era conducted surveys in 2011, 2014, and 2016 to determine the impact that potential Internet regulations may have on their investing activities. Our findings have been consistent across all three studies. They are summarized below.

Investors are chilled by regulatory ambiguity and would reduce their capital investment if countries introduce Internet regulations that reduce their investment viability or return.

Exhibit 13

% Investors Perception of Legal Environment Impact on Investing

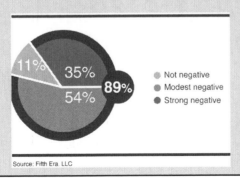

Source: Fifth Era, LLC

Investors are concerned by some potential regulations in areas including:

- **Legal Encroachment:** Globally, investors view the legal environment as having the most negative impact on their investing activities, with 89% of the investors surveyed saying it had a modest or strongly negative impact (see Exhibit 13).

- **Regulatory Ambiguity:** In every country surveyed, a large majority of investors say that they are uncomfortable investing in business models in which the regulatory framework is ambiguous. Of the worldwide investors surveyed, 75% held this view.

- **Security/Surveillance:** 81% of investors would not invest in Internet businesses if government agencies could confiscate properties without court orders.

- **Taxation:** 80% of investors are concerned that countries may apply tax rules that make them subject to double taxation.

- **Freedom of Expression:** 79% of investors are uncomfortable investing in countries where freedom of expression is restricted or highly regulated.

- **Amount of Damages Uncertain:** 78% of investors would not invest in Internet business models in which the amount of damages (in the event of liability) is uncertain or not tiered or staged in relation to the various levels of violation.

- **Law Enforcement Access to Data:** 78% of investors would be deterred from investing in Internet businesses if user data could be disclosed to law enforcement without following international baseline standards.

- **Third-Party Liability:** 71% of investors are uncomfortable investing in Internet businesses where the intermediaries could be held liable for third-party content or actions.

- **Data Storage In-Country:** 67% of investors are uncomfortable investing in Internet businesses that are legally obligated to store user data on servers located in the same country where users are located and/or build their own data centers locally in each country of operations.

- **Site Blocking:** 62% of investors are uncomfortable investing in digital content intermediary businesses (online platforms allowing uploads of user-generated content, including music and video) that would be required by law to run a technological filter on user-uploaded content.

- **Content Removal:** 71% of investors are uncomfortable investing in Internet businesses that would be obligated to remove content upon receiving a request from an organization, private or government entity, without a court order.

- **Traditional Telecom Regulations:** 63% of investors are uncomfortable investing in Internet/mobile businesses where regulators are applying traditional telecom regulations to new mobile and over-the-top services.

- **Mobile Regulation Reductions:** 77% of investors say that if a country adopts policies aimed at reducing regulations for the mobile apps ecosystem, this would increase their interest in investment in Internet businesses in that country.

More generally, investors say that they would reduce their capital investment in countries that introduce new Internet regulations that may limit the ability of Internet businesses to be attractive investment candidates. As a result, government lawmakers should engage investors in their decision making early to ensure that regulations are not introduced without a full understanding of the potential adverse consequences to investment activity.

Source: Le Merle, M., Davis, A., & Le Merle, F. (2015). The impact of Internet regulation on investment. Fifth Era LLC.

The wildcards are each possible. The Fifth Era is not assured. Humankind holds its own destiny in its hands, and some critical choices are upon us regarding our collective future. In particular, governments can kill our future of innovation and transformation by choosing a world of economic balkanization, government-sponsored cybersecurity attacks, and excessive and suffocating regulation.

However, we believe we will avoid all three wildcards and that the Fifth Era will be our future. It is just a question of how fast it will take to come to pass—and how long the time of transition will last.

In the next part of this book, we turn to the scale of the wealth being created by Fifth Era disrupters, who is playing for that wealth, and who is sitting on the sidelines—so far at least.

Part 2 | Wealth Creation in the Fifth Era

Chapter 4
The Greatest Wealth-Creation
Opportunity Ever?

Innovation is the specific instrument of entrepreneurship. The act
that endows resources with a new capacity to create wealth.

—Peter Drucker

We stated in earlier chapters that times of transition between eras are enormous wealth-creation opportunities. This is the result of two factors. On the one hand, disruptive innovations open up new sources of opportunity that did not exist before. On the other, they may shift the playing field such that the capabilities and assets that allowed players to win in the past may no longer be the ones that define success in the future. As a result of these two factors, the subsequent era's wealth creation is potentially open to new players who are bringing new capabilities and resources that are more relevant in the next era.

We see this quite clearly in the transition phases between prior eras. For example, the Agrarian Era was dominated by people who owned land because land gave the opportunity to deploy the new agricultural innovations of the time. In the shift from the Agrarian Era to the Mercantile Era, wealth was captured by merchants who understood how to use the new technologies of international travel (the age of sail, navigation, and so forth), how to identify goods that could be sold profitably in other geographies, and how to trade for those goods. City-states that were built upon this mercantile mindset were where these new entrepreneurs clustered together and accumulated their wealth. They were good places to be a merchant. In this transition, we see wealth shift from one group of players with a certain type of capabilities and assets to another who had attributes that better suited the new times.

In this chapter, we will demonstrate that the coming Fifth Era and the time of transition that we are living through is already the greatest wealth-creation opportunity that the world has ever seen.

Three Observations about Today's World

As we explore the transition phase we are in and assess the wealth creation that is resulting, we should first make three observations about the state of the world today.

First, the population of the world is larger than it has ever been. When we went through prior transitions between eras, the earth supported a much smaller human population, in the hundreds of millions, or in the case of the Industrial Era, in the small number of billions. But, this era that we are now entering sees the world with a combined global population approaching eight billion. What this means is that we have a much larger population of people passing through the transition (see Exhibit 2 in Chapter 1: The Population Curve).

Second, the economic activity of the world is also higher than it's ever been, as witnessed through measures, such as GDP per capita. The absolute economic output of the world has never been larger. This means that the economic profit pools being impacted are larger than existed in the past.

Exhibit 14

World GDP Per Capita Adjusted for Inflation

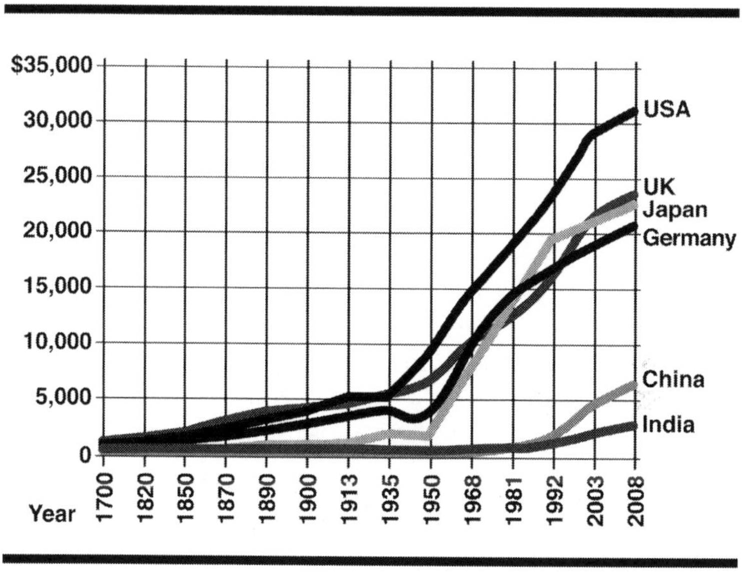

Source: Angus Maddison

Finally, the world is more globally connected than it was in the past. Earlier we described how globalization was not necessarily a one-directional phenomenon, and we walked through the wildcard of how balkanization between continents and nations might unwind globalization. However, the world is still a more global place today than it has ever been. Addressable markets are larger, and new technologies have the opportunity to capture more profits by serving more people from the moment that they launch.

These simple observations—the population is larger than ever, the combined economic activity is greater than ever, and globalization is at an unprecedented level—are all reasons why we expect that the current time of transition should represent a larger wealth-creation opportunity than at any time before.

The world is passing through its greatest wealth-creation phase to date.

World's Most Valuable Companies Are Fifth Era Companies

The world's most valuable companies are already Fifth Era companies. The majority of the large companies in the world today are public companies, and as a result, their market capitalizations can be measured in the public markets. For the last hundred years or so, the most valuable companies on those lists were industrial companies and resource-heavy companies. They were the big industrial companies, such as General Electric and IBM in America. They were the large resource-heavy companies, such as the oil majors, including Exxon-Mobil and Shell, and more recently the Chinese oil company Sinopec. And, they were also the large multinational financial institutions that supported the Industrial Era and the trading and financial activity that the large companies were engaged in. And so, we saw on the lists the names of banks, like Bank of America, Royal Bank of Scotland, and Wells Fargo, and more recently Chinese banks, including Industrial and Commercial Bank of China, China Construction Bank Corporation, and Agricultural Bank of China.

Today, if we review a list of the world's most valuable companies by market capitalization, it looks markedly different. Take a look:

Exhibit 15
Largest Companies by Market Capitalization

Symbol	Company	Cap Rank on 2/28/17	Market Cap on 2/28/17
AAPL	Apple	1	718.7
GOOGL	Alphabet	2	584.2
MSFT	Microsoft	3	494.4
BRK-A	Berkshire Hathaway	4	423.4
AMZN	Amazon.com	5	403.2
FB	Facebook	6	391.7
XOM	Exxon Mobil	7	337.2
JNJ	Johnson & Johnson	8	332.5
JPM	JPMorgan Chase	9	323.6
WFC	Wells Fargo	10	290.3

Source: Dogsofthedow.com

No less than five of the six most valuable companies in the world today are technology companies, and additional companies fill out the list farther down the rankings beyond the top ten. Not only are the most valuable companies in the world technology companies, but most of them are new Fifth Era technology companies. The list includes Apple, Alphabet/Google, Microsoft, Amazon, and Facebook, of which most of them have more of a leg in the new Fifth Era world—the connected, interactive world as described in Part 1—and have relatively a smaller foot in the Industrial Era computing phase, although Apple and Microsoft began in the computer phase of the Industrial Era.

Indeed, when we look at Apple or Microsoft, they increasingly put more emphasis on the Internet and the new, emerging computer and content technologies, and they have begun to scale back and even exit the legacy computing environments of the past where they were first founded. Amazon, Alphabet/Google, and Facebook conversely are all children of this transition phase, and their businesses are almost entirely built upon new, emerging, and disruptive technologies.

These companies, Apple, Alphabet/Google, Microsoft, Amazon, and Facebook, in particular, have risen to become the most valuable companies in the world, and that's not simply because they have large revenues and profits pools today. Of course, they do. Apple has revenue of $214.2B, driving an incredible annual net income of $45.7B. Alphabet, driven by the Google search machine, has revenue of $89.7B and net income of $19.5B. The second reason why these companies are so valuable is because the world's investors view them as the companies best positioned to capitalize on the coming Fifth Era, which is evidenced in their high P/E ratios and the expectations of a great deal of future growth that these companies will capture.

These companies are, for the most part, also at the frontier of many of the disruptive innovations described in part 1. We see Apple exploring new data analytics and artificial intelligence algorithms, continuing to expand its content portals and payments approaches, and exploring self-driving vehicles and other coming disruptive innovations.

Alphabet has gone so far as to split its company essentially into two parts, with Google continuing to operate the very large but relatively new businesses that it built as part of the digital revolution. Those new businesses include areas such as search, video sharing through YouTube, email through Gmail, and so on. Meanwhile, the other half of Alphabet is entirely focused on creating businesses in the areas of new disruptive innovations that we described above. Alphabet is making substantial investments and inroads into areas as diverse as self-driving vehicles, robotics, artificial intelligence, genomics, and more, and calls them "moonshots."

These observations—that the world's most valuable companies are today Fifth Era technology companies, that the public market investors expect these companies to show the greatest growth of the large companies in the world, and that these companies in themselves are betting so heavily on new areas of disruptive innovation—should not be taken lightly. But, this is the first of many observations we'll make about why this transition phase is already proving to be the world's greatest wealth-creation opportunity.

World's Richest People Are Fifth Era Entrepreneurs

There are a number of respected journals and publications that create lists of the world's richest people. A hundred years ago, those lists were dominated by the landed gentry, financiers, and early industrialists, like the Carnegies and Rockefellers. Today, if we look at the list of the world's richest people, we see a very different story.

Exhibit 16

Forbes **Listing of the Top 25 Wealthiest People in North America**

Rank	Name	Net Worth $B	Core Business
1	Bill Gates	$84.40	Microsoft
2	Warren Buffett	$73.30	Berkshire Hathaway
3	Jeff Bezos	$69.90	Amazon.com
4	Mark Zuckerberg	$55.00	Facebook
5	Larry Ellison	$50.10	Oracle
6	Michael Bloomberg	$44.80	Bloomberg LP
7	Charles Koch	$44.50	Koch Industries
8	David Koch	$44.50	Koch Industries
9	Larry Page	$39.20	Google
10	Sergey Brin	$38.40	Google
11	S. Robson Walton	$33.00	Wal-mart
12	Jim Walton	$32.90	Wal-mart
13	Alice Walton	$32.70	Wal-mart
14	Steve Ballmer	$29.50	Microsoft
15	Sheldon Adelson	$29.40	Las Vegas Sands Corp.
16	Jacquelin Mars	$28.60	Mars inc.
17	John Mars	$28.60	Mars Inc.
18	George Soros	$25.20	Soros Fund Management LLC
19	Phil Knight	$24.50	Nike
20	Michael Dell	$20.50	Dell
21	Laurene Powell Jobs	$20.50	Apple, Disney
22	Len Blavatnik	$19.90	LyondellBasell, Rocket Internet, Warner Music
23	Paul Allen	$19.60	Microsoft, investments
24	Charles Ergen	$17.90	Dish Network
25	Carl Icahn	$16.80	Icahn Capital Management

Sources: *Forbes*, Fifth Era, LLC

In order to answer the question, "How did these people make the ranks of most wealthy in North America?" we assessed the degree to which their wealth is derived from entrepreneurialism, by taking advantage of disruptive technologies, and/or by benefiting from the formation of global markets and the trends of globalization. When looked at through this light, we discover that 17 of the top 25 are entrepreneurs themselves, 18 of the top 25 own or run technology-enabled businesses (this includes companies like Wal-Mart that have utilized new technologies across their businesses), and 22 of the top 25 have benefited from the globalization of markets as their businesses have become multinational or global in scope.

As you can see, the vast majority of the 25 richest people in North America are also recent additions to the list. A large proportion are first generation technology entrepreneurs with no inherited wealth to speak of.

Not only is the arrival of the Fifth Era wealth very clear in the rankings of the wealthiest people in North America, but also the absolute scale of that wealth is quite remarkable. When we combine the wealth of the top 25 people in North America, we have a total in excess of $900 billion, which represents about 1% percent of the total wealth of all North Americans. In the next chapter, we will explore just why it is that these Fifth Era entrepreneurs are able to capture and hold such a large proportion of the wealth that their businesses have created.

The first way that we measured this wealth-creation opportunity was by looking at the most valuable companies in the world, and this second view, where we look at the wealthiest people, also confirms that we seem to be in the middle of the greatest wealth-creation opportunity the world has ever seen.

Just a North American Phenomenon?

The prior two charts are, of course, dominated by the North American story. All five of the technology companies ranked today on the list of the top six global companies by market capitalization are US companies and indeed all five of them are headquartered in the Western United States, with two of them in Seattle and three of them in the San Francisco Bay Area. When we look at the list of the world's richest people, not surprisingly, we see a similar phenomenon where most of those people are also US-based and clustered on the West Coast.

To some, this will not be a surprise. America was built by those who took risks in the face of religious persecution in Europe. While many stayed, a few left. Every American family has one of the few - a pioneer or entrepreneur - in its past. We were all immigrants (and in our case, we are first generation Americans), and those who chose to come to this continent did so because they were the risk-takers, they were the entrepreneurs, and they were willing to bet to win—and were willing to fail too. American blood pulses with entrepreneurial vigor.

Is this just a North American phenomenon? The answer is no. Exhibit 17 shows the rankings of the wealthiest people in China.

Exhibit 17
Ranking of China's Richest People

Rank	Name	Net Worth $B	Core Business
1	Wang Jianlin	$31.60	Dalian Wanda Group
2	Jack Ma	$28.40	Alibaba Group
3	Ma Huateng	$24.20	Tencent Holdings
4	Wang Wei	$16.50	SF Express
5	William Ding	$15.10	Netease
6	Wang Wenyin	$14.70	Amer International Group Co. Ltd.
7	Robin Li	$12.80	Baidu
8	He Xiangjian	$11.50	Midea Group Co. Ltd.
9	Hui Ka Yan	$9.80	Evergrande Real Estate
10	Yao Zhenhua	$8.50	Baonang Group
11	Lei Jun	$8.40	Xiaomi
12	Zhang Zhidong	$8.10	Tencent Holdings
13	Yang Huiyan	$8.00	Contry Garden Holdings
14	Liu Qiangdong	$7.40	JD.com
15	Zong Qinghou	$7.20	Hangzhou Wahaha Group
16	Zhang Shiping	$6.60	China Hongqiao Group
17	Liu Yongxing	$6.60	East Hope Group
18	Xu Shihui	$6.60	Dali Food Groups Co.
19	Li Shufu	$6.30	Volvo
20	Guo Guangchang	$6.20	Fosun International
21	Wei Jianjun	$6.00	Great Wall Motor
22	Xu Chuanhua	$5.80	Transfar Group
23	Pan Zhengmin	$5.70	AAC Technologies Holdings
24	Yan Zhi	$5.60	Zall Group
25	Lu Guanqui	$5.60	Wanxiang Group

Sources: *Forbes*, Fifth Era, LLC

Some three decades ago, the Chinese government began to bring the Chinese economy into a new model. "Capitalism with Chinese characters" was the phrase used to describe this new model. In order to effect this change, the Chinese government began to privatize state assets and looked for talented entrepreneurs who could accept the responsibility for leading and improving large components of what before had been state-owned industries. That early transition of wealth in the Chinese context gave rise to the first generation of Chinese billionaires, many of whom are still represented on the list of the wealthiest people in China. These are not by definition Fifth Era entrepreneurs—they are, rather, beneficiaries of the shift in the Chinese economic model.

However, when we look through the top of the Chinese wealth list, we also see the founders of Chinese Fifth Era companies, including Jack Ma of Alibaba, Ma Huateng of Tencent, William Deng of Netease, and so on—all of which are new, disruptive Fifth Era companies.

Just as we saw in the American context, the wealthiest people in China are increasingly being dominated by those entrepreneurs who are taking on the responsibility for commercializing and monetizing the disruptive innovations of our time. These are the Fifth Era entrepreneurs, and in China, they, too, are able to hold onto a large proportion of the wealth-creation opportunities that their companies are monetizing. In the case of China, 24 of the wealthiest 25 are entrepreneurs, 18 of 25 lead technology-enabled businesses, and 21 of 25 are already benefiting from global markets. China, too, is seeing the new disruptive innovations and the coming Fifth Era, creating a generation of wealthy citizens as some take the opportunity to become entrepreneurs driving innovation-based companies.

China is becoming a land of innovators, entrepreneurs, and investors just as much as the US has been to date.

Just for the fun of it (we are, after all, dual US and UK citizens), we also took a look at the list of the wealthiest people in the UK. Here we do not see the arrival of Fifth Era entrepreneurial wealth in the way that we have demonstrated in the US and China. Here the list is much more dominated by the legacy of the industrial era, with the majority of wealthy people being landed gentry, financiers, and inherited wealth.

Exhibit 18
Ranking of UK's Richest People

Rank	Name	Net Worth $B	Core Business
1	David & Simon Reuben	$15.70	Reuben Brothers
2	Hinduja Family	$15.30	Hinduja Group
3	James Ratcliffe	$9.00	Ineos Group
4	Charles Cadogan	$6.90	Diversified
5	Ian & Richard Livingstone	$5.90	London & Regional
6	Joe Lewis	$5.60	Tavistock Group
7	David & Frederick Barclay	$5.10	Diversified
8	Bruno Schroder	$5.10	Schroders
9	Richard Branson	$5.00	Virgin
10	Philip & Christina Green	$4.80	Arcadia Group
11	Laurence Graff	$4.60	Graff Diamonds
12	Michael Platt	$4.50	Bluecrest Capital Management
13	Clive Calder	$4.50	Zomba Group
14	James Dyson	$4.20	Dyson
15	Denise Coates	$3.70	Bet365
16	Andrew Currie	$3.00	Ineos Group
17	John Reece	$3.00	Ineos Group
18	Bernard Ecclestone	$2.90	Formula One Group
19	Anthony Bamford	$2.90	JCB
20	Peter Hargreaves	$2.80	Hargreaves Lansdown
21	Michael Ashley	$2.70	Sports Direct
22	Robert Miller	$2.60	DFS
23	Sunil Vaswani	$2.40	Stallion Group
24	Farhad Moshiri	$2.40	Arsenal F.C.
25	John Caudwell	$2.20	Phones4u

Sources: *Forbes,* Fifth Era, LLC

Let's leave it to the reader to decide what to make of this observation. But, we don't believe it undermines the observation that the greatest wealth-creation opportunity in history is giving rise to the wealthiest people in history. For our part, we believe that the UK is well-positioned to become an active player in the Fifth Era. The UK has:

- Outstanding researchers and scientists in world-class centers of innovation
- Great education for technologists across most areas of disruptive innovation

- A long history of entrepreneurialism and new business success stories to inspire the next generation
- Access to capital and to financial markets
- An excellent business and regulatory environment in which to locate large and small technology companies
- A substantial local economy
- English-speaking people well-positioned to serve international markets
- A special UK:US relationship that seems to attract leading US companies to base themselves there

We think that the UK can be an important global innovation cluster and launching point for international technology companies that want to be close to the European continent but don't want to be burdened by the excessive and counterproductive policies and regulations of a worryingly bureaucratic European government. It will be interesting to see if the UK can seize the opportunity provided by Brexit, and conversely, whether Europe can avoid the wildcard of excessive regulation and policy, encouraging its technology entrepreneurs to go elsewhere, including to the UK.

When regarded through the lens of the world's most valuable companies and the lens of the world's wealthiest people, we are seeing the accumulations of the largest pools of wealth that the world has ever seen, and this is just at the top of the pyramid. To this, can be added the many hundreds of financiers: venture capitalists and private equity investors who have also built fortunes by investing in these same companies and entrepreneurs. We can also add the increasing ranks of wealthy employees at these companies who have participated in initial public offerings and have seen their options and stock greatly appreciate. Other entrepreneurs, investors and employees who have sold their emerging companies through mergers and acquisitions with larger corporations, have also become wealthy in the process.

In the next chapter, we will explore how the dynamics of wealth creation are quite different in this Fifth Era than they were in the Industrial Era.

Chapter 5
Wealth Creation Being Secured Early

Early to bed and early to rise makes a man healthy,
wealthy, and wise.

—Benjamin Franklin

Let's now explore how and where this wealth is being secured. In this chapter, we will show that the dynamics of wealth creation have shifted in this time of transition, that entrepreneurs seem able, at least in this timeframe, to hold onto a larger portion of their wealth than was historically the case, and that the highest returns are being captured by those investors who invest early. We will also see that the private phase for some of the most successful Fifth Era companies is being extended, and they're taking longer, by design, before choosing to become public companies. As a result, by the time the public market investors get to play, the largest portion of the wealth has already been spoken for.

Technology Entrepreneurs Benefiting

As demonstrated by the list of the US' most valuable companies and North America's and China's richest people, these entrepreneurs are demonstrating the ability to commercialize new disruptive innovations and to still retain a substantial portion of their company's equity in this timeframe.

Through multiple phases of funding, we see entrepreneurs continuously diluted as larger and larger amounts of capital enter their businesses. However, the costs of building these new companies have been shrinking quickly as a result of globalization and the arrival of new technologies that make building products and serving markets cheaper. In addition, valuation dynamics have been accelerating so quickly that the equity percentage that entrepreneurs are able to hold, even after a decade of multiple rounds of financing, is often still very substantial.

We live in a time in which the rewards of entrepreneurialism seem to be within reach for those who take the risks and manage the process of company formation and growth effectively. We think this is appropriate. Innovation rests on the shoulders of those few who will step up and take the risks—they deserve to be rewarded—and without them we would all be the poorer.

Every day we are thrilled by the optimism, ambition, and courage of these entrepreneurs, and it is exciting to see them begin to fill the ranks of the most wealthy in countries on both sides of the world.

Venture Capital Returns Highest Early

When we view the same dynamic of early-stage funding and wealth creation through the lens of the returns on investment for professional venture capital fund investors, we see confirmation of the wealth being secured and created early. (see Sidebar 4: What Is a VC, Angel, GP, and LP?) This provides an overview of important terminology that we will use here and through the rest of this book regarding what it means to be a venture capitalist (VC), angel investor, general partner (GP), and limited partner (LP).

Cambridge Associates is a company that tracks the returns of venture capital investors, and in Exhibit 19, you can see how those returns vary across the different phases of venture capital, from early- to mid-stage to late-stage. To this chart of Cambridge Associates data, we have added the typical return secured in the public markets for the New York Stock Exchange, NASDAQ, and the S&P 500.

Exhibit 19

Cambridge Associates and Public Market Returns Chart

Index	5-Year	10-Year	15-Year	20-Year	25-Year
Cambridge Associates LLC U.S. VC Index	17.69	10.98	2.89	33.72	24.35
– U.S. VC - Early Stage Index	19.40	11.10	1.88	58.65	32.32
– U.S. VC - Late/Expansion Stage Index	15.10	13.16	5.09	10.53	13.29
– U.S. VC - Multi-Stage Index	15.86	10.12	4.41	12.39	14.36
Barclays Government/Credit Bond Index	3.09	4.61	5.36	5.60	6.44
Nasdaq Composite Index	14.30	7.94	1.54	7.72	10.94
Russell 2000 Index	11.73	6.55	6.51	7.95	10.57
S&P 500 Index	13.34	6.8	3.96	8.14	9.90

Note: As of September 30, 2016
Source: Cambridge Associates LLC, Barclays, Dow Jones Indexes,
Frank Russell Company, Standard & Poor's, Thomson Reuters Datastream
and Wilshire Associates, Inc.

Across multiple periods, we see that the early-stage (including formation to seed stage) venture capital returns are the highest of any asset class and that the venture capitalists have been able to capture net returns to their investors in the 20% to 30% range by investing very early in emerging companies that are participating in the Digital and Biotechnology Revolutions.

When we look at the Cambridge Associates US Venture Index, which combines all stages of venture investment, we see a net return of 24.3% over the last 25 years. The venture capital return from early-stage investments in the same timeframe is 32.3%. The venture returns drop to 13.2% in the late/expansion stages. This is not that much higher than the 10.9% that the NASDAQ Composite Index earned. In short, the venture capitalists got their highest return on their capital by investing early and securing positions in emerging disruptive technology companies at the beginning of those companies' lives.

Later in this book, we will explain why most venture capitalists choose to invest more of their limited partner capital in later stages rather than earlier-stage rounds despite this return disparity. Suffice to say here that the general partners of a venture capital firm are economically rational in their behaviors.

Sidebar 4: What Is a VC, Angel, GP, and LP?

To help readers who may be new to the field, we define venture capitalist (VC), angel investor, general partner (GP), and limited partner (LP) as follows (Sources National Venture Capital Association (NVCA) and Angel Capital Association (ACA)).

Venture Capitalist (VC)

Venture capital firms are professional, institutional managers of risk capital that enable and support the most innovative and promising companies. This money funds new ideas that could not be financed with traditional bank financing, that threaten established products and services in a corporation, and that typically require five to eight years to reach maturity. Venture capital is quite unique as an institutional investor asset class. In venture capital, when an investment is made in a company, it is an equity investment in a company whose stock is essentially illiquid and worthless until a company matures, five to eight years down the road. Follow-on investment provides additional funding as the company grows. These "rounds," typically occurring every year or two, are also equity investments, with the shares allocated among the investors and management team based on an agreed "valuation." But, unless a company is acquired or goes public, there is little actual value. Venture capital is a long-term investment.

Angel Investors

Angel investors are accredited investors who invest their own money and expertise in high-growth, private start-ups. In the United States, to be considered an individual accredited investor, the person must have a net worth of at least one million US dollars, excluding the value of their primary residence, or have income of at least $200,000 each year for the last two years (or $300,000 combined income if married) and have the expectation to make the same amount in the ensuing year.

> ### General Partners (GP)
>
> A general partner represents a class of partner in a partnership. The general partner retains liability for the actions of the partnership. Historically, venture capital, angel co-investment, and buyout funds have been structured as limited partnerships, with the firm as the GP and limited partners (LPs) being the institutional and high net worth investors that provide most of the capital in the partnership. The GP earns a management fee and a percentage of gains.
>
> ### Limited Partners (LP)
>
> A limited partner is an investor in a limited partnership. The general partner is liable for the actions of the partnership while the limited partners are generally protected from legal actions and any losses beyond their original investment. The limited partner receives income, capital gains, and tax benefits but does not directly make the investment decisions of the partnership.

Angel Returns Confirm This Phenomenon

Now turning to angel investors who are individual investors that help launch companies in their formation, seed, and early stages, we see a similar phenomenon. Robert Wiltbank, who was a professor at Willamette University's Atkinson Graduate School of Management where he ran the Willamette Angel Fund, analyzed angel investor returns. His research demonstrates that they typically earned a return of 22% in his 2016 assessment and 29% in his 2007 work across their investments in emerging technology companies. Recent research by professors Josh Lerner and Antoinette Schoar, at Harvard and MIT, respectively, confirm these findings. Lerner and Schoar find that angel investor returns exceed venture capital returns in some cases (see Sidebar 5: The Expected Returns of Angel Investors in Groups).

When we combine these observations from North American venture capital and angel investor returns, we see that both demonstrate that the highest returns are created and secured very early in the lifecycles of these disruptive Fifth Era companies.

Sidebar 5: The Expected Return of Angel Investors in Groups

Angel investors back more than 71,000 businesses each year in the US and many hundreds of thousands more around the world. These are most frequently technology-enabled businesses and are seen to be important drivers of innovation, GDP, and job growth by most countries worldwide. And while there is little academic research into angel investors, those researchers in this space have found:

- The return to angels investing in groups is viewed as attractive and perhaps as high as net annual internal rate of returns (IRRs) in the mid-20%s.

- In their ground-breaking 2002 research, Mason and Harrison in the UK show that angels have a significantly lower number of exits (a positive exit being a sale or public offering of a company in most cases) that return no capital (39.8% as compared to 64.2% for VCs), have a larger number that return modest IRRs, and have roughly comparable proportions of exits showing IRRs exceeding 50% (angels 23.5% of deals, VCs 21.5% of deals).

- Angels achieve their returns with relatively low failure rates and lots of modest returns, adding to the return of the relatively infrequent large exits. Mason and Harrison also showed that technology deals outperform non-technology deals in their period of assessment.

- Professor Wiltbank, working with the support of the Kauffman and Angel Capital Education Foundations in the US in 2007 and the British Business Angels Association in the UK in 2009, showed that:

  - Angels can expect an average return of 2.6 times their investment in 3.5 years for a 27% IRR in the US.

  - Angels can expect an average return of 2.2 times their investment in just under 4 years for a 22% IRR in the UK.

- Geoff Roach (2008) conducted focused research on the world's largest angel group, Keiretsu Forum. His assessment of annual angel investor returns provides very similar findings. By 2008, the annualized returns for the cohorts in the Keiretsu Forum portfolio were 2000 – 20.38%, 2001 – 21.32%, 2002 – 28.24%, 2003 – 26.20%, 2004 – 32.46%, 2005 – 14.55%, and 2006 – 20.13%

- Those returns arrive over a 3- to 5-year timeframe with a tail of investments that may take longer to realize.

- The successful exits tend to be less skewed than the venture capital experience, but nonetheless, a majority of the total return is still returned by a small number of highly successful outcomes.

- While this makes the average angel return attractive, it also implies that a significant number of angel investors may still have portfolios that do not perform, and, in fact, many angels do not see a return of capital.

- The most practical way for an angel to raise the likelihood of capturing the angel return is to ensure they are highly diversified in terms of the number of companies they hold in their portfolio, and if they have a specific industry or sector focus, then at that specific level too.

- Angels understand both the attractive returns possible and the need for diversification. However, angels are limited in their ability to achieve diversification. In practice, most invest in far fewer early-stage technology companies than preferable.

Source: Le Merle, M., & Le Merle, L. (2016). Capturing the expected returns of angel investors in groups—Less in more, diversify. Fifth Era LLC.

So, angels too confirm this truth. The wealth being built by the transition to the Fifth Era is being captured in the early phases of business formation. This is not really a surprise. We already showed that entrepreneurs are at the heart of this transition. Entrepreneurs are changing the world, and angels perch on their shoulders.

Companies Private for Longer

The private investment phase has also been extended for longer time periods. Investors have been investing more and more capital into increasingly larger funding rounds of so-called "unicorns." Venture capitalist Aileen Lee in a November 2013 TechCrunch article termed the class of private companies with valuations of more than a billion dollars as "unicorns," in light of the fact that they're supposed to be mythical creatures that don't exist in the real world. In the past, venture capital-backed companies would have moved quickly to exit, either by being acquired by large corporate players or, in a minority of cases, by seeking an initial public offering in the public markets. Today, private companies can stay private longer, receive the capital they need, and potentially become unicorns.

How has this happened? What's changed since the dotcom crash of 2001–2002 is that the top-tier venture capitalists have raised ever-larger funds and have chosen to put that money to work by investing directly into their own portfolios of emerging technology companies, thus fueling continued expansion and postponing the IPO and the company's arrival into the public markets.

As an example, Uber, which is today valued at around $62.5B, has raised approximately $8.8B of capital, an amount unheard of two and three decades ago. Of course, today we see many unicorns of the Fifth Era company variety, not only in North America but elsewhere. In the North American context we currently count 229 unicorns, including companies like Airbnb ($30B) and Palantir ($20B).

This postponement of the listing of these Fifth Era technology-enabled companies into the public markets has also given rise to great consternation in those public market investors that would normally have funded and been the big beneficiaries of IPOs. The large Wall Street sources of capital and institutional investors have increasingly explored ways to put some of their own capital to work in the earlier phases of wealth creation. They've done this indirectly by putting larger amounts of capital as limited partners into the leading venture capital firms, and they've also done it directly by participating in expansion capital rounds directly as investors.

Public Company Model Threatened?

As noted in Part 1, we do expect the Fifth Era to see a challenge to the dominant Industrial Era models of large corporations funded by public markets. Already by 2016, the number of publicly-traded companies in the United States has fallen 46% from a peak of 8,025 in 1996 to 4,333 in June 2016.

Exhibit 20
Number of US Public Companies

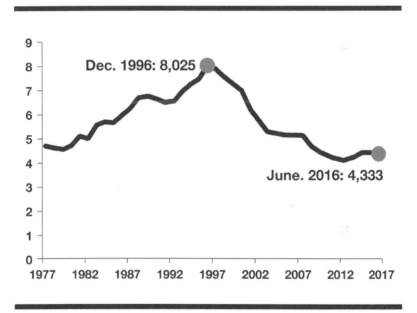

Source: JP Morgan Asset Management

This reduction in the number of publicly-traded US companies is not only a result of concentration, as the established players have acquired smaller companies, but it is also a result of the arrival of a large number of private companies and the exiting from the public markets of smaller old Industrial Era companies that can no longer support the growth and profitability required to stay public on the major stock exchanges. Fifth Era companies seem to prefer the private model.

What will be the new equilibrium between public and private in the next handful of decades? We are not sure, but any shift as significant as the one seen in the last ten years brings massive dislocation to the sources of capital for corporate financings and, as noted, has also been accompanied by a shift in how wealth is captured by investors.

In this chapter, we demonstrated that the world's greatest wealth-creation opportunity is being secured early and is increasingly in the hands of private companies and private investors. While most of our observations are being made from a United States' viewpoint, we believe that these underlying phenomena are true elsewhere too. The Chinese experience seems to confirm these observations with a rising number of unicorns and well-capitalized private investors. The European context is less clear with very many fewer unicorns and less private market investment in the region.

The question this then raises is "Who is participating in this wealth creation—and perhaps as importantly—who isn't?"

In the next chapter, we answer this question.

Chapter 6
Most People on the Sidelines

It is not in the stars to hold our destiny but in ourselves.

—William Shakespeare

In the prior two chapters, we established that this transition phase and the arrival of the Fifth Era represents the greatest wealth-creation opportunity that the world has ever seen and that this wealth creation is being secured early, primarily by the entrepreneurs who are taking advantage of new disruptive innovations and by the angels and venture capitalists who are backing them. We also described how this is in marked contrast to the way the financial markets worked in the past, where the majority of large company financing occurred in the public markets, through equity and debt financing rounds. We left the last chapter, asking, "Who is participating in this wealth creation—and perhaps as importantly—who isn't?"

A Handful of Technology Entrepreneurs

How many people in America are choosing to be tech entrepreneurs? Here, no comprehensive database exists. However, we can estimate an answer to the question by looking at the number of companies that the venture capitalists and angels are backing each year. Amongst the venture capital community, the NVCA (2017) shows that the US venture capital community backed 7,750 companies in 2016, of which only 2,340 were first-time venture fundings (the rest being follow-on financings). If we say on average that each of those first-time companies may have had two co-founders and perhaps ten or so early employees at the stage preparing for these first rounds of venture capital, then we might have a population of perhaps 30,000 or so technology entrepreneurs and early employees who every year are being backed in the US by venture capitalists.

Angel investors do a better job, backing roughly 71,110 companies per year, according to Jeffrey Sohl at the University of New Hampshire Center for Venture Research. If we make the assumption that at the time angels back these companies, they average two co-founders and three employees, then we have a total technology entrepreneur base of perhaps another 355,000.

Combining these two numbers (and, yes, of course, there is some overlap, but let's try to create the biggest number we can by ignoring it) of 30,000 and 355,000, we have a total of 385,000 US technology entrepreneurs—co-founders and very early employees. Given that the US has a total population of 319 million and a working population of 156 million, we can see that even being generous we can't find more than 0.2% of the working population choosing to join the ranks of technology entrepreneurs each year.

While we don't have similar statistics for all the countries in the world, and in this book we do not attempt to estimate a similar global statistic, the data that we have seen from the OECD, World Bank DataBank, and European Eurostat databases all seem to move in the same direction as these US findings. Very few people anywhere in the world are active technology entrepreneurs.

Very Few Venture Capitalists and Angels

A second question, then, is "If they're choosing not to be technology entrepreneurs, how many of them are investing in entrepreneurs?" In the United States, we have on the order of 12.5 million accredited investor-qualified households, according to the SEC's qualifications. The current definition of an accredited investor in the US requires that you have $1 million of net worth, excluding your primary residence, or $200,000 of income in each of the prior two years or $300,000 of income when combined with your spouse, along with the expectation that your income stream will continue at least at this level. How many of these 12.5 million households are actively backing Fifth Era companies and positioning themselves to benefit from this massive wealth creation?

The Center for Venture Research at the University of New Hampshire found that in 2015 only 304,930 accredited investors were active angel investors in early-stage companies. That means only 2.4% of qualified households have chosen to be active angel investors in Fifth Era companies (probably a few less since some households house two or more angel investors—like ours).

In the United States, meanwhile, we have 898 venture capital firms, according to the NVCA. On average, each of those firms is run by between two and five general partners, meaning that we estimate a total general partner base in the venture capital industry in America of no more than 4,500.

As a result of combining these two numbers, we can see that perhaps 309,500 US investors are focused on investing in Fifth Era disruptive technology companies. A tiny percentage (2.5%) of the 12.5 million Americans that could be direct investors in early-stage technology companies are choosing to be so.

Most US accredited households are not acting as entrepreneurs of, and are not investing in, new Fifth Era companies.

As with technology entrepreneur statistics, we don't have similar venture capital and angel investor statistics for all the countries in the world, and we believe that in most countries these types of investors are not tracked at all. The exceptions, in some parts of Europe and Asia where associations and agencies are beginning to gather venture capital and angel data, certainly confirm these findings—and initial estimates suggest an even smaller percentage of local market accredited investors are actively investing as VCs or angels. As more comprehensive statistics are gathered, it will be interesting to compare the US with other countries. However, we feel comfortable in extending the US finding to a worldwide finding: a tiny percentage of those who could be are choosing to be active investors in private technology companies as venture capitalists or angel investors.

An Imbalance in Gender Participation

Are men and women acting similarly? At a macro-level the answer is yes. Most men are not participating in the disruptive innovation companies as entrepreneurs or investors, and this is true for women too. But, taking a closer look, we find it is even worse when gender is brought into view.

As entrepreneurs, men outnumber women by a substantial degree. The Ewing Marion Kauffman Foundation, which researches start-ups and angel investing, found that women opened 36.8% of US businesses in 2014 and that this has been dropping from being closer to the long-term average of 40% (2014).

In 2016, TechCrunch conducted an analysis of women in venture capital and the impact it has on the female founders. They found that only 7% of the partners in the top 100 venture firms are female (54 of 755) and that only 38% of the top 100 firms have any female partners at all.

TechCrunch also analyzed 54 active corporate venture funds and 101 incubators and accelerators, and found that only 12% of the senior and partner roles were held by women. TechCrunch then analyzed funding activities of venture capitalists and found that they invest in very few companies that have at least one woman founder:

- 12% of venture rounds and 10% of venture dollars globally between 2010 and 2015 went to start-ups with at least one female founder.
- 17% of seed rounds and 15% of seed dollars globally between 2010 and 2015 went to start-ups with at least one female founder.

Marianne Hudson, the president of the US Angel Capital Association, estimates that around 22% of angels are female, a percentage up from single digits a decade ago. At Keiretsu Forum, the founder and CEO, Randy Williams, has a global leadership team that is 25% female chapter chairpeople and presidents, and female angel membership has been increasing steadily. However, Marianne and Randy believe this is still much lower than desirable, and we agree.

According to the Bank of Montreal's Wealth Institute, 51% of American personal wealth is now controlled by women, and that proportion is expected to increase (2015). The Boston Consulting Group estimates that 30% of the world's wealth is owned by women—and that 44% of wealthy women are self-made, 27% inherited their wealth, and 24% received it from their spouse and/or in divorces, leaving 5% from other reasons (2016).

What accounts for this disparity between the percentage of entrepreneurs and investors (venture capital partners, corporate venture partners, incubator and accelerator leaders, and angel investors) and the wealth that women own? We are not sure; however, we see no reasons why this could not dramatically shift. In America, women drive the philanthropy of the nation, so why shouldn't they drive entrepreneurialism and investment too?

The women of the world are our most valuable underutilized resource as we enter the Fifth Era.

A Minority of Public Markets Investment

The final lens to look through takes us to public market portfolios where we consider the percentage of US investments being directed into technology companies through the public markets. Of course, this is not a proxy for the early-stage investment opportunity because most of the public market technology companies are either old Industrial Era computing companies, such as IBM and AT&T, or they are the handful of Fifth Era technology companies that have already chosen to go public, such as Apple, Amazon, Alphabet, Facebook, and Microsoft. But, it does at least illustrate that US investors might be seeking technology participation even if they did not have access to early-stage private investment opportunities.

When we look at the typical portfolio of American investors, we find that only a small proportion of it is invested into technology companies. Many financial advisors encourage clients to avoid "high-risk" technology stocks—in many cases these advisors are rewarded for not losing capital and don't see any change in their compensation if their clients get a high return—they are paid fixed fees or transaction fees but not a percentage of capital increases. As a result, they may encourage their clients to be risk-averse and to "hoard" their capital in investments that may have a low, or even negative, real return but also may have a low risk of capital loss. In our opinion, hoarders and active early-stage investors are polar opposites. Hoarders hold to themselves for fear of loss while active early-stage investors back others for the opportunity to gain. Of course, we are active early-stage investors ourselves.

This last lens seems to confirm the other lenses. A small percentage of the investable assets of American investors is today being channeled into early-stage private technology companies, and accredited investors are under-represented in terms of their investments in this opportunity. Meanwhile, the public markets don't provide access directly into the most attractive early-stage disruptive innovation and Fifth Era companies.

In summarizing this second part of our story, we have already established in Part 1 that the world moves through eras and that disruptive technologies are what create the transition phases in which a prior era transitions into a new one, and we provided a long list of evidence that we are now living through just such a disruptive innovation transition phase as we exit the Industrial Era and move into the Fifth Era.

In this second part of our book, we demonstrated that this time of transition is the greatest wealth-creation opportunity the world has ever seen and that the wealth is being secured early by the entrepreneurs and investors that are taking advantage of these new disruptive innovations and turning them into companies ready to bring their products and services to market. However, most people, most workers, and investors are on the sidelines, with very few of them choosing to be entrepreneurs and very few of them being direct investors in early-stage technology companies.

If you are one of the people who is not yet participating and does not have a strategy to build your fortune in the Fifth Era, then Part 3 of this book is written specifically for you.

Part 3 | How You Can Build a Fortune in the Fifth Era

Chapter 7
Know Your Own Objectives, Capabilities & Assets

The most difficult thing in life is to know yourself.

—Thales

Most people have not yet chosen to participate in the Fifth Era and in the wealth-creation opportunity that it represents. As discussed in the previous chapter, in the US only about 0.2% of people are each year becoming technology entrepreneurs, and perhaps only 2.5% are active investors (VC and angel). Before we suggest you jump in, we encourage you to read through this final part of our book. In Chapter 7, we outline some questions you should ask yourself to better understand what you have as raw material for the game ahead. In Chapter 8, we detail many of the ways to play and some of the indicators that would allow you to decide which options best fit your self-evaluation from Chapter 7.

Know Yourself

As Thales of Miletus, an Agrarian Era Greek philosopher and one of the seven sages of Greece, is believed to have said, "The most difficult thing in life is to know yourself." In the specific case of determining how to build your fortune in the Fifth Era, it is important to begin with just that task because there are a lot of ways to play and who you are may naturally make it easier to decide, in Chapter 9, how you should play the game.

We suggest you answer three questions that we will delineate in this chapter:

1. What are your personal investment objectives?

2. Who are you or could you be?
3. What other leverageable assets do you bring with you?

What Are Your Personal Investment Objectives?

In asking this first question, we don't want you to worry about specific outcomes that you might be seeking; for example, technologies and innovations you want to be involved with; numbers of companies you want to start, work with, or be invested in; impacts on society you want to help drive; capital you wish to deploy; rates of return you target and absolute wealth-creation results in terms of cash returns over time; diversification of your portfolio; and so forth. While these are all important matters, they are not the ones to differentiate between the options we discuss in Chapter 8.

Rather, we would suggest that you explore your desire to participate in the innovation process itself and your tolerance for acting quickly versus watching and waiting. Implicit in this is your tolerance for failure and everything that goes along with it.

To these we will add, later, the roles you are best suited to play, given your capabilities and an inventory of your other leverageable assets, since these also may differentiate between the options we present in Chapter 8.

In this time of transition, there are advantages and disadvantages to each option, and intuitively some may appear preferential, given your answers to this first perspective on who you are.

The First Mover

Are you a person that needs to be at the front and involved at the outset? Do you want to break new ground, explore uncharted territory, and/or participate in the innovation process itself? Do you embrace the unknown and the chaotic and unsettling times when dead ends and long diversions are more the norm and efforts constantly need to be adjusted, redirected, relaunched, pivoted, and so on? Are you willing to suffer a score of failures yet still get up? Can you cope with loss after loss and still look for the silver linings—the lessons that failures teach? Are you obstinate and opinionated? Do you refuse to take no for an answer? Do you believe that you and your team will succeed regardless of the adversity all around you? Are you willing to be made a fool of as others say you must be out of your head? Do you trust your judgments and decisions?

If you answer "yes" more often than "no," then maybe you are a first mover. Most of us are not.

Watch and Move Fast a Little Later

While there is some truth to the notion of first mover advantage, it can be very fruitful to watch and move fast a little later. Netscape may have invented the browser, but Microsoft ate it for lunch in round two. We were investors in Inktomi, which ruled search in the early dotcom period—Google came along and where is Inktomi today? We invested in Google as soon as the IPO allowed it: we had learned our lesson.

Some people just don't like being first, but they are happy to watch the first movers, see what is getting traction, and then move quickly. Sometimes very quickly indeed. And they are brutal in being willing to shoulder aside the first movers: take their place, push them out the way, beg, borrow, and steal their innovations and creations.

It is a lot of work to do this well. Indeed, it may be more work than just being a first mover because there is so much more ground that needs scouting out. But, conversely, you can more easily avoid the bleeding edge of innovation and failure. And this strategy can allow you to make a lot more bets. Instead of owning one or two things that you have to drive to completion, watching and moving fast a little later can also be accompanied with multiple small bets in those things that seem to have traction. Then you can double down on what begins to move fastest. It's also harder for people to make fun of you: you may not always get it right and sometimes you may miss out on something big, but at least you can always point at all the first movers who look even sillier in the abundance of their failures. Your failures were carefully considered ones.

If this intuitively feels more comfortable and a better fit for you, note it down.

Rely upon Advisors to Determine Your Strategy

Maybe this whole chapter is already difficult for you. You don't like the vagueness of it all. You don't want to make your own decisions around how quickly to move. All this talk of failure, losses, embarrassment, and humiliation is just not your cup of tea. You don't want to be in the chaotic world of innovation and disruption yourself. You do want to play—sort of—but you would prefer that someone else is actually out on the field. You'll put on the team jersey, shout loudly from the stands, but you don't really want to run all over the field and get constantly tackled, knocked down, and trampled on. You would rather the players play, and you spectate. And if you have a great commentator to listen to, that would be good too.

Don't worry, there are plenty of people out there looking to help you if you feel this way. You may be passive, but you can still play through others.

Don't Play-Let Others Capture the Value

What's wrong with not playing at all? Most people don't. In the Agrarian, Mercantile, and Industrial Eras only a few capitalized on the disruptive innovations and secured the benefits, one way or another. In fact, of millions of people, perhaps only a few thousand, did things really well in the first couple of eras—maybe a few tens of thousands in the most recent.

That's all right then. You are being no different from most people during most times of transition. Not playing is the norm during era transitions. Most people, through inertia, continue to live by the mindset of the last era and don't jump onto the bandwagon of what is coming next.

But, what's a little different this time around, as we will show, is that the very disruptive innovations that are enabling an entirely digital world of distributed innovation are also enabling a much larger number of people to get access to the possibility of playing and to actually play, in one way or another.

The Fifth Era is coming, disruptive innovation is the leitmotif of our times. Don't get to the end of your road, look back, and regret that you let it all pass you by unless you are really sure this is your preferred objective.

Who Are You or Could You Be?

In Chapter 8, we will profile the various options for getting access to and participating in early-stage private disruptive innovation companies. Some of you may already have well-developed capabilities in innovation, supporting innovation, and/or investing, including in proximate areas that might allow you to expand into this emerging area. So, who are you or could you be as an investor?

Innovator

Are you already an innovator? Do you work in a center of innovation—academic, corporate, or government-owned? Are you a scientist, researcher, or someone with access to these people? Do you understand the new technologies and their potential? Are you in the flow of innovations and are you involved in the dialog regarding which have most promise and where? Can you understand the language of the scientific and development community working in the area? Do you know what deserves to be a patent, and what patents are already in place that would block an innovation? Do you know who else is working on this and where they are in terms of their progress? Is science, broadly defined, your thing?

Entrepreneur

Maybe you don't consider yourself an innovator, but for sure you know how to commercialize innovations. You have the first-mover sensibility even more than the innovators. You are willing to place the biggest bet of all—all of your own time—behind your beliefs. You may have done it before and been successful, in which case the very fact you would do it again speaks volumes. Maybe you have tried and failed, but you just keep on getting up again. First-time entrepreneurs beware. Very few people have the entrepreneurial capability. As we already estimated, in US venture capitalists and angel investors combined we find 0.2% or 308,500 as investable technology entrepreneurs and early-stage employees each year—of which perhaps half are not Americans but rather immigrants, trying to live the American dream.

Valuable Service Provider

Now the bar drops greatly. Are you a valuable service provider? Do you have capabilities that innovators and entrepreneurs need? Are you a lawyer, IP attorney, financier (see below), governance expert, fundraiser par excellence, marketer, PR person, go-to-market channel expert, technology consultant, human resources and recruiting expert, accountant, bookkeeper, and so forth? Do you have something that a small company needs, regardless of whether they have the cash to afford you? If so, that will play across several of the options of Chapter 8.

Investor (Passive)

Do you have investable capital that you can afford to lose? In the US, today, you should probably be an accredited investor—although as we shall see our nation's regulators will be very happy to let you invest (at your own risk, of course) even if you are not. Notwithstanding this, do you have more than $1 million in net worth, excluding your primary residence, or income of $200,000 in each of the last two years or $300,000 with your spouse? Are you willing to put perhaps 10% of that at risk in illiquid, high-risk investments that you may never see the benefit of and at least probabilistically may suffer 100% loss of capital on?

Investor (Active-Value-Added and Capital)

If you said yes to one of innovator, entrepreneur, and/or valuable service provider, AND yes to investor (passive), then you can also check this box too.

Now that we are clear on what core capabilities you have, or are confident you could have, let's wrap up by seeing what other leverageable assets you bring with you.

What Other Leverageable Assets Do You Possess?

This book is written primarily for individuals. However, we still need to ask whether you control a company and its assets or you have a significant influence over the same? If so, this could be a very important element of your wealth-building strategy for the Fifth Era.

Company Assets

There are many things that new disruptive innovation-based companies don't have that they need to get quickly in order to succeed. Larger established companies often have exactly the things that start-ups need and can act as kingmakers. As a result, your company may be able to help emerging companies succeed, and if you can control that process, you may be able to benefit directly—assuming you don't do anything you should not and you don't put your own interests ahead of your employers, shareholders, etc.

If you do own or control an existing business, a partial list of leverageable assets to consider as you go into Chapter 8 would include:

- Insights into technologies, patents, existing solutions, etc.
- Your own innovators who can help emerging company innovators do their work
- Existing products and services that can be the beneficiaries of new innovations
- Existing customers who can pilot and eventually roll out new innovations
- Sources of traffic to cross-market to or use as early adopters
- Go-to-market capabilities in terms of channels, distributors, partners, and so on
- Service capabilities to support new innovations when they go live
- Regulator capabilities to get innovations approved and navigate the issues associated with getting them successfully into new and existing markets
- International footprints to take innovations to other markets

If you have some or all of these capabilities, you may be well-positioned to ensure emerging companies that you back have a higher likelihood of succeeding.

Personal Capital

We have already noted that this is high-risk, illiquid investing and that you need to be thoughtful about how much capital you will deploy to this asset class since total capital loss is possible—some investors will lose every investment they make just by the laws of statistics. As a rule of thumb, an accredited investor should probably pencil in 10% of their investable assets at most into this asset class until they get into a category where they have already put more into "safe" asset classes than they will ever need.

Another way of thinking about this question of how much capital you need is to consider how much you need to make enough investments to have a diversified portfolio. If that magic number is 40 for example, then even in a crowdfunding option you will need at least 40 x $1,000 or $40,000 (e.g., AngelList, the leading US crowdfunding platform, has a current minimum investment size of $1,000). For angel investments, the minimum is typically $25,000 (and sometimes more) so that you need $1,000,000 to get to 40 investments. Another option is angel funds, which may allow you to get diversification at a lower total capital investment. But, it certainly helps to have sufficient risk capital in most of the options we will describe.

Relationships

In our own rights, we all have our own relationship network. For some people, depending upon how they spend their time, they may have a large and powerful personal relationship network that may be the greatest asset of all for determining the success of an early-stage company and innovation. As we will describe in Chapter 8, being able to influence a network to get behind a company and an innovation can be worth multiples of the invested capital—opening the door to have a company license a technology, getting other investors to invest, persuading an influential customer to pilot a product or service and give it a good reference within the industry, getting key opinion leaders, technology writers, and analysts and journalists to say great things, and being able to influence regulators to allow a disruptive innovation to have a period to prove itself.

Time

Do you have time? This is a major factor that helps differentiate between the Chapter 8 strategic options. Some people don't have time. They may have a full-time job, they may have too large a portfolio of other priorities, they may simply have a lower tolerance for work— they prefer to use their time in non-work related ways. Some of the options require a great deal of time. On the other hand, some of the options require no time to speak of.

Risk Tolerance

We already touched upon this, but it is very important as you go through Chapter 8 to have a sense for where you stand on failure. Failure is consistent across early-stage disruptive innovation-based businesses, and almost every option we will present has at least a 50% failure rate or more. Some people just don't want to lose more than half the time. Very few people enjoy losing anything like that frequently.

If you have read through this chapter, really thought carefully about who you are and who you want to be, and inventoried what you bring to the party, then you are ready for the next two chapters and constructing your own strategy for building a Fifth Era fortune.

But first, take a minute to fill out your personal scorecard. We also encourage you to go to the book website to take a survey online and indicate your interests for participating in the Fifth Era. Go to: http://BuildYourFortuneInTheFifthEra.com

Personal Scorecard

Objectives	Rank	Notes
First Mover	☐	
Fast Follower	☐	
Rely on Advisors	☐	
Don't play *Are you sure?*	☐	

Capabilities (existing or could be)	Check all that apply	Notes
Innovator	☐	
Entrepreneur	☐	
Valuable Service Provider	☐	
Investor (Passive)	☐	
Investor (Active)	☐	

Other Leveragable Assets	Check all that apply	Notes
Corporate *Make a list*	☐	_____
Personal Capital	☐	_____
Relationships *Make a list*	☐	_____
Time *Hrs/week*	☐	_____
Risk Tolerance	☐	_____

Chapter 8
Review the Ways to Play

It is our choices . . . that show what we truly are,
far more than our abilities.

—J. K. Rowling

Since you have read this far, we anticipate that you are now ready to decide how you will take advantage of this wave of disruptive technologies to build your own fortune. If so, you are ready for this next chapter. Here we will review the ways to play and indicate the capabilities required and the pros and cons of each.

Our first two options are those in which you jump in with all of your time and effort as either a technology entrepreneur founding a Fifth Era disruptive technology company (Option 1) or as an early employee (Option 2). We would be remiss not to start by considering these two options because they are the two that created the wealthiest people in the world, as demonstrated in Part 2 of this book. Of course, they are not options for most of our readers.

- Option 1. Technology Entrepreneur
- Option 2. Employee of a Fifth Era Company

We then look at two options that most people think are going to allow them to invest in early-stage disruptive companies: being a general partner (Option 3) or being a passive investor in a venture capital fund (Option 4). As we will show, these can be very attractive options, but in practice very few people have the opportunity to do either.

- Option 3. Active Investor: Venture Capital Fund
- Option 4. Passive Investor: Venture Capital Funds

The good news—there are three additional options that are open to almost anyone who wants to play. These three options are being an active angel investor (Option 5), being a passive investor in an angel co-investment fund (Option 6), or being a crowdfunding investor (Option 7).

- Option 5. Active Investor: Angel Investor
- Option 6. Passive Investor: Angel Co-Investment Funds
- Option 7. Crowdfunding Investor

Finally, we review two options that have a great deal of promise for those who would like to cast a wide net and have the time and commitment to being a provider to Fifth Era companies. Option 8 reviews how you might create an incubator or accelerator while Option 9 is the somewhat less demanding option of providing professional services to the companies in exchange for some combination of cash and equity.

- Option 8. Provider of an Incubator and/or Accelerator
- Option 9. Provider of Professional Services to Fifth Era Companies

We briefly describe each option, review the pros and cons, and summarize for whom each option is best suited.

Option 1. Technology Entrepreneur

In Part 2 of this book, we estimated that there are around 308,500 investable technology founders and very early employees funded each year in the US. While that only represents 0.2% of the working population, it is possible that this option would be the correct one for you.

Right now, the newspapers are full of stories of how young technology entrepreneurs have launched companies, grown rapidly, and become fabulously wealthy in short timeframes. Larry Page and Sergey Brin met at Stanford in 1995 when Sergey was assigned to show Larry around campus during his application process. They began to work together from their dorm room on the challenge of creating a better search engine for the world-wide web with the mission of organizing the world's information and making it universally accessible and useful. An angel investor, Andy Bechtolsheim, who had been a co-founder of Sun Microsystems, was so impressed he gave them their first $100,000, and Google was born. Later, the two were funded by Michael Moritz of Sequoia and John Doerr of Kleiner Perkins Caufield Byers. Today, just over 20 years on, Alphabet/Google is one of world's most valuable companies, and Larry and Sergey are both on the list of the world's wealthiest people.

In 2005, we were fortunate to meet three company founders: Kevin Bruner, Dan Connors, and Troy Molander. The three were all technologists, innovators, and entrepreneurs. They and a team of others were working together in the advanced technologies group at LucasArts, the video game division of George Lucas' company, when their latest game, *Sam and Max: Freelance Police*, was cancelled. They decided to create their own company, Telltale Games. Their mission was to create a digital entertainment breakthrough by bringing great stories to the world in an episodic, downloadable format. We gave them the initial capital they needed and joined the company as chairman and board director. Today, Telltale is the worldwide leader in episodic video games, and the team is deservedly wealthy as Telltale moves into unicorn status. All in just over ten years.

Both the Google and the Telltale founders achieved amazing things in a very short timeframe. But, they had great capabilities, vision, and entrepreneurial zeal.

There are great resources for figuring out if you have what it takes to be an entrepreneur too. We like one that tests your "EQ—Entrepreneurial Quotient" that was developed by Guy Kawasaki, who was an early Apple evangelist and is now an executive fellow at Haas Business School at UC Berkeley. We suggest that would-be technology entrepreneurs take the test; there is an online and an offline version at Guy's site:

guykawasaki.com/whats_your_eq_e/

Guy also has a very helpful online course that we are impressed by:

www.udemy.com/entrepreneurship-course-by-guy-kawasaki/

After taking the EQ test and the online course, we think you may be better prepared to assess your true readiness to be a technology entrepreneur. We wish we could give you a better way to assess if this option is right for you. If we could bottle and sell the spirit of the entrepreneur, we would be the wealthiest of people. But, we don't know the magic formula.

Pros and Cons

The pros are very real if you can make a success of this option. While partners at AT Kearney, we were once working on setting up the private banking strategy for Bank of America, and the executive chairman of the private bank told us a secret over dinner one night:

About the 3 Levels of Wealth in America

The first level of wealth is primarily corporate and professional. Enough to have a lovely house, a vacation home, good schools for the kids, a nice car or two, enough for most reasonable hobbies, and so forth. Get a job, be good at it, rise through the ranks, and become a partner in a firm or a senior executive of a corporation.

The second level of wealth is held by the American small business owner. There are a lot of them—tens of millions, in fact. And the more successful ones have tens of millions of net worth though often a lot of it is tied up in their business. Their businesses are not always sexy: local dry cleaners with multiple outlets, automobile franchise dealers, people with a successful plumbing business in a big city, and so on. While it is true that a few very well paid professional investors and corporate executives with large option and share grants also get into this second level, they are the exceptions. For the most part, the second level is dominated by small business owners and entrepreneurs.

And then there is the third level of wealth. The people we all read about. Worth hundreds of millions. Like the list we had from *Forbes* earlier in this book. Who are they?

In some regards, they are the same as the second level of wealth—the small business owners and entrepreneurs. But, they got lucky. They owned their own small businesses, and those businesses became big ones.

They took the risk of entrepreneurship, and they were the few for whom it paid off big.

Of course, being a technology entrepreneur who will operate successfully at the very frontier of human understanding is a much tougher task than being a small business owner launching your own pizza restaurant or home-cleaning business. You not only need to be good at running a business—you need to figure out what that business is as you commercialize new and unproven disruptive innovations. It seems that technology entrepreneurs are even fewer in number than regular entrepreneurs.

We can't give you a great deal of advice about making the decision to become a technology entrepreneur. We know a lot about helping technology entrepreneurs create their business plans and raise their funding, as well as what comes after they are funded. But, actually being a technology entrepreneur? We never have been one and don't know how to be one.

We would say, caveat emptor on this option. If you bet all of your time on one high-risk venture, expect that it will fail, however good you are. The statistics say that most do fail. But, of course, as a true entrepreneur you did not hear that: you know you won't fail.

And as a technology entrepreneur, don't forget to build a great team of people who are better than you. But, then again, our experience is that true entrepreneurs believe there is no one better than them for the opportunity they are pursuing.

We hope many of you will read this option and say it is for you. Entrepreneurs are the few that make the world better for the many. If just a handful of the readers of this book decide to plunge in and become entrepreneurs, it will have been worthwhile writing it.

At this point we should also note that disruptive innovations are also being applied to solve social issues and make human activities more sustainable. The twin movements of social entrepreneurialism and sustainable business are driving a great deal of very positive change and are creating powerful new ways to achieve positive outcomes for humankind. While not the focus of this edition, we plan to return to this theme in a subsequent book. And it is a good reason for many to choose the path of technology entrepreneur.

This is a good option for you if your scorecard was checked:

1. First Mover (or maybe Fast Follower)
2. Innovator or Entrepreneur
3. Preferably some of the other boxes—Time and Risk Tolerance, of course; maybe Relationships. Capital and Corporate Assets are beneficial but not required.

Option 2. Employee of a Fifth Era Company

Most emerging companies begin with one or two co-founders (sometimes more). Those founders split the common stock at the outset. Then as they raise a little formation capital, they usually take the step of hiring a handful of like-minded people who are employees rather than founders but still are very early in the game.

An early employee can expect stock and/or options too. Often it is quite a lot until organized investors, like angels and venture capitalists, become investors in the company. At that point, equity will be strictly rationed, and the valuation will have gone to a place where an employee will typically not receive more than a handful of basis points (tenths of one percent).

However, there is a window of opportunity that makes this a good option for some people. That window is between the founders forming the company and the first real investors coming on board. During this timeframe, an employee with the right skills and insights into the founders and their vision can often negotiate a good deal and secure enough in equity to become wealthy if the start-up succeeds (and dilution by capital raised in subsequent rounds is controlled).

We met Omid Kordestani in 1998 when, with Michael DeVico and his team, we were helping set the online strategy for Bank of America. Omid had arrived in California at the age of 14 after spending his early years in Iran. He attended San Jose State University, was an engineer at HP, and then graduated with an MBA from Stanford Graduate School of Business in 1991. After periods as an employee at 3DO and Go, Omid joined Netscape with responsibility for OEM sales, which is when we met with him as he tried to sell Bank of America on the notion of having a search capability on the front page of www.bankofamerica.com. Then, in 1999, Omid became an early employee of

Google, and for 10 years he worked in Google sales, becoming SVP of worldwide sales and field operations. By the time Omid left Google in 2009, he was a billionaire. Today, he is executive chairman of Twitter and has been voted one of the Top 100 people who shape our world by *Time Magazine*.

Omid is a good example because he did not hit his home run straight away. Being an employee at HP, 3DO, Go, and Netscape put him into the right space and built out his capabilities, experience, and network. They set him up for success at Google. And Omid is not alone. People like Marissa Mayer from Google, who went on to become CEO of Yahoo, Jack Dorsey, who tuned his dispatch technology skills at another company we backed called Dispatch Management Services (DMSC) before founding Twitter and Square, and Sheryl Sandberg, who began her career at McKinsey, moved to Google, and is today COO of Facebook, all took this strategy of joining a fast-growth disruptive company once it had passed its inflection point but early enough to provide confidence that a share and option package might prove to be sufficient to build a fortune, or two.

It really helps to know great founders for this option. The best founders are much more likely to be able to raise capital, especially if they have been backed by top-tier investors in their past ventures. Coming on board early as a serial entrepreneur that prepares their next big thing can make a lot of sense. Conversely, joining an unproven first-time founder in their venture is generally not going to be a smart way to play this option.

Pros and Cons

The big pro of this option is that it allows you to be an equity holder of a Fifth Era company even if you are not an entrepreneur yourself and would not be able to play Option 1. You will learn a lot and may one day be able to create your own start-up after experiencing the employee role in one or two ventures led by others. If you have the technical and functional skills needed in a start-up setting, this can be a reasonable way to keep yourself employed.

The main negatives are the same as in Option 1. You are betting all your time on one specific idea, but this time you are also betting on a specific founder(s). Are you confident they are investable and likely to make a success of this? Your future depends upon it.

This is a good option for you if your scorecard was checked:

4. First Mover (or maybe Fast Follower)
5. Innovator or Entrepreneur-in-the-making—but not quite there yet
6. Preferably some of the other boxes—Time and Risk Tolerance, of course; maybe Relationships. Capital and Corporate Assets are beneficial but not required.

The next two options are those which most people think are going to allow them to invest in early-stage disruptive companies: being an active investor in a venture capital fund (Option 3) or being a passive investor in venture capital funds (Option 4). These can be very attractive options, but in practice very few people have the opportunity to do either.

Option 3. Active Investor: Venture Capital Fund

Direct investment into Fifth Era companies in their earliest stages when the returns are likely to be the largest seems to be a good option, based upon the words we have written to this point. The expected returns are high—perhaps the highest of any current asset class in America. The risk is substantial, at 50% to 70% failure on average, but there is plenty of evidence that 10% of the investments will return 5 times or more, and, in so doing, those handful will drive your average return in the mid- to high-20% annual returns. There is real risk that if you don't invest enough times, you may expose yourself to the risk of total capital loss, but if you invest in 48 or more companies, you seem to have around 95% likelihood of earning the asset class return while even at 24 investments you are at a 90% probability level. And, since you are an investor and not an entrepreneur or employee, this option gives you the chance to broadly diversify. You can invest in as many companies as you wish—assuming you have the capital, deal flow, ability to do the due diligence, and time to support the companies once you invest in them.

This was the first option we went after when we were first working for Bankers Trust Venture Capital Fund while at business school in the 1980s, next seeking to launch AT Kearney Ventures in the 1990s, and then working with Monitor Ventures in the early 2000s.

Back in the 1980s and 1990s, the venture capitalist options really were the best way to back start-ups. But, is that still the case? Who invests in start-ups today and how do you become one of them? That is not quite as obvious as you might think. In fact, venture capitalists rarely invest in start-ups these days (see Sidebar 6: Do VCs Back Start-Ups?). Over the last few years they have become more focused on the rounds of capital following the early stage. Today, venture capitalists put most of their capital to work in the mid- and late stages of venture capital funding. They do this for good reasons.

What we are observing now is that 80% of formation- and seed-stage start-up funding in America is provided by angel investors with most of the rest coming from venture capital funds and a small but growing portion coming from incubator and accelerator funds and crowdfunding.

Sidebar 6: Do VCs Back Start-Ups?

The traditional model of start-up funding has always held that investors in technology companies at inception include the entrepreneurs themselves, their friends and families, and angel investors, who are willing to invest their own money into the new companies. Later, early- and late-stage VC funds may become investors in these start-ups, but they only do so once the company has matured to a point that it is considered investable by the VC (see Exhibit 22). However, in the main, people simplify this multi-part funding cycle into a simple premise—VCs back start-ups.

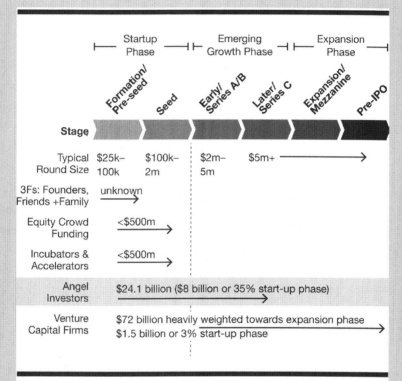

Exhibit 21
Equity Capital For Technology Entrepreneurs

Sources: Jeffrey E. Sohl, Robert Wiltbank, Ian Hathaway, Crowdnetic, ACA,
NVCA, Pricewaterhouse Coopers, Dow Jones Venture Source, Fifth Era, LLC

But, this has been changing very rapidly, and, as a result, the conventional wisdom is now misleading.

According to the most recent NVCA 2017 Yearbook, VCs have effectively stopped seeding most start-ups in the US:

For the full year 2016, US VCs invested $69 billion but only into 7,750 companies.

Of this $69 billion, the majority went to mid-stage and pre-IPO companies and not start-ups. Only approximately $1.5 billion or 3% of the venture capital funding was in the seed or earlier rounds when companies were in their initial start-up phase. Venture capitalists backed fewer seed and earlier companies in 2015 than in any year since 1995.

In short, today US VCs are focusing their efforts and capital on emerging-growth companies, and very few start-ups receive any funding from VCs until they can justify valuations in the double digit millions of dollars – typically a series A round early stage investment. VCs simply do not deploy material capital into the start-up phase of a company's lifecycle in the US (formation- and seed-stage funding). Instead, US technology companies seeking VC capital will need to have moved a long way beyond a business strategy—they will have established their company, formed their founding team, built their initial products, perhaps begun to serve customers in the marketplace, and might even be generating substantial revenue—before a VC will consider them for an investment. VCs back very few start-ups.

What Changed?

After the 2008 crisis, US VCs were confronted by a substantial shakeout and a flight of capital to leading firms. The best VCs got much larger while others, in the face of this flight of capital, ceased to invest and instead focused on their existing portfolios. Many VCs went out of business altogether. As the NVCA 2016 Yearbook points out:

The number of VC firms in the US is today only 898, down from 1,009 in 2005.

Interestingly, while the number of firms has declined, the money managed has increased. The average firm now manages $243.6 million, and the largest fund raised was a whopping $4.3 billion.

In 2015 alone, the VCs raised an additional $41.6 billion, which they needed to invest.

This trend of fewer funds and fewer professionals managing ever-larger sums of money gives rise to some simple consequences:

VCs prefer to put larger amounts of money into each deal that they back. In addition, while the larger VC firms are backing more companies, they are doing so in later stages. Instead of investing in start-ups at the formation and seed stages, they are investing in those companies later in their lifecycles.

Many VCs are putting the bulk of their money to work in well-established later-stage growth firms or as pre-IPO capital, essentially what used to be known as expansion capital investing.

Furthermore, many VCs are also participating in "non-venture-related investments," including investing in debt, buyouts, recapitalizations, secondary purchases, IPOs, and public companies, such as PIPES (private investments in public entities), investments which the proceeds are primarily intended for acquisition, such as roll-ups, change of ownership, and other forms of private equity that are not even captured in the statistics of the NVCA.

In short, and with a few exceptions, VCs have become expansion capital investors, rather than start-up investors. And this is unlikely to change given the massive amount of capital that is today managed by US VCs. If not VCs, then who does back start-ups?

By the relative numbers it can be seen that angel investors are much more important for most companies in their start-up phase of life compared to VCs who, for the most part, only invest in angel-backed companies once they have significant traction that justifies larger investment rounds (see Exhibit 23). The angels of the US are seeding most US technology start-ups.

Exhibit 22
Angels Back Most US Start-ups

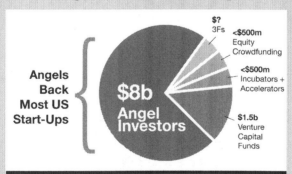

* Formation and seed rounds – estimates from sources
Sources: Jeffrey E. Sohl, Robert Wiltbank, Ian Hathaway, Crowdnetic, ACA, NVCA, Pricewaterhouse Coopers, Dow Jones Venture Source, Fifth Era, LLC

Source: Le Merle, M., & Le Merle, Max. (2016). Do VCs back start-ups? Ensuring start-ups are backed in an innovation cluster. Fifth Era LLC.

Notwithstanding this migration of venture capital firms away from the early stage of investment, Option 3 is to become a general partner in a venture capital fund. This way you make the investment decisions yourself (with your fellow general partners), you get to invest other people's capital (your limited partners), and you get the upside, or around 20% of the upside, on every dollar you invest (this is called "carried interest" or "carry," and is defined as a share of the profits of an investment paid to the general partner in excess of the amount that they contributed to the partnership).

You also get to spend 2% to 2.5% of the fund capital every year in the management fee, which covers whatever expenses you have, including your own salary, for the life of the fund (typically ten to thirteen years since most venture capital funds have a ten-year life with the option of up to three one-year extensions) unless you put in a novel term where you only get the management fee on a reducing-capital base. If you can raise $100m, that means $2m a year to spend on your firm. Of course, if you raise $1 billion . . . just do the math.

Sir Michael Moritz is perhaps the world's foremost venture capitalist and someone we have worked with, both at Gamefly and Xoom, both of which were backed by his firm Sequoia and general partners, including Roelof Botha. It is instructive to take a look at Sir Michael's rise to prominence. He was born in Wales and attended Christ Church, Oxford, in the 1970s, where he studied history, followed by an MBA from The Wharton School. His first career was as a journalist, including at *Times Magazine*. Steve Jobs famously picked Sir Michael to write the story of the development of the Mac and is quoted as saying that he should be "Apple's historian." By the early 1980s, he was head of the San Francisco bureau of *Time Magazine*, covering Silicon Valley and the technology companies. After writing books on Apple and Chrysler, he decided to change professions and joined Sequoia in 1986. His history of investments in early-stage disruptive companies is one of the best in Silicon Valley, and he has backed a long list of spectacularly successful companies, including Google, LinkedIn, PayPal, Yahoo, YouTube, and Zappos. Sir Michael was knighted by the Queen in 2013 and remains as chairman of Sequoia today.

Well, of course, Sir Michael is an exception. Good venture capitalists and venture capital firms are few and far between. As NCVA tells us, there are only 898 venture firms in all of the US, and while they have billions to invest, it's extremely hard to become one of them. The typical venture firm only has between 2 and 4 general partners, and those are the people who raised the fund capital in the first place. They don't typically invite others to join them mid-fund and may not be able to, depending upon what the fund documents say.

Actually, it is almost impossible to become a top-performing (top quartile) venture capitalist. You likely begin as a technology entrepreneur, investment banker, or perhaps management consultant. Once you have done very well in one of those professions, you join a venture firm as a lowly associate (and they don't have many of those positions either). There you do a few years of excellent work, including eventually finding some great investments for your firm. At last you are ready to become a general partner, except that the firm almost certainly does not want any more general partners (there are exceptions but rare). So, now you either leave to create your own small venture capital fund, leveraging your established venture firm track record, or you create a micro fund or become an active angel investor.

Pros and Cons

The pros can be unbelievable. The world's largest venture capital funds have billions of dollars to invest each year. And the general partners who benefit from most of the 20% carried interest shared between them can become billionaires, especially if they back a few Fifth Era unicorns that achieve liquidity events, such as IPOs or corporate acquisitions.

The daily life is not easy. The firm has to wade through thousands of technology entrepreneur teams and pitches for each one that gets the thumbs up. The average venture capital firm only invests perhaps 5 or 6 times a year, but each month hundreds want to meet, and even more are met at industry events of one sort or another. It is a lot of work to evaluate the most promising proposals, it is a lot of work to negotiate and do the deal, and it is even more work to shepherd each company along post-investment. Even still, the track record is that around 50% fail even with all the best hard work of great venture capitalists. Failure comes with the territory. And failure comes first—successes take longer. Most successful venture capitalists will tell you that they live day-to-day lives full of intense stress and worry.

Adjusted for the risk, it turns out that most venture capital funds don't actually create economic value. The top quartile can do outrageously well. But, the average firm is nothing to shout about. The reason we have so few venture capital firms is that the bottom quartile typically go out of business once their LPs see the results; they just won't invest in the next fund and the general partners have the unfortunate task of overseeing a declining portfolio of investments for a few more years, knowing they will probably never raise another fund, given their poor track record.

Sorry to be the bearer of bad news, but for most of the 12 million of you reading this book who are accredited US households and who want to play but have not yet started, this is not really a viable option for you. Unless you are one in a million or so.

This is a good option for you if your scorecard was checked:

1. Fast Follower (or maybe First Mover)
2. Innovator, Entrepreneur, or Investor (Active)
3. Most of the leveragable asset boxes, and if you checked Corporate, maybe you can be a Corporate VC.

Option 4. Passive Investor: Venture Capital Funds

So, you have come this far, and you now realize that Options 1, 2 and 3 will not work for you. You don't want to be full-time, you don't want to do the hard work, you don't want to trust your own decision-making, and you don't want to put in the long hours to take a company from first funding to eventual exit—and maybe all of the above.

Option 4 is the first of a couple of passive investor options in which you give your capital to someone else (the general partners) who will manage it for you and make sure it is invested in early-stage companies with the profile that you want, if you can find a fund manager who shares your interests. In the case of Option 4, you are becoming a limited partner in a traditional venture capital fund or are an investor in a fund of funds, or you are making secondary market investments in venture capital-backed companies.

In the case of most early-stage venture capital funds, the general partner charges you an annual management fee for doing all the work (typically 2.0% to 2.5%) and shares in the profits by taking typically 20% of the carried interest. Now you have to pay attention here: there are all sorts of small print that can get into the fund documents, like the right to recycle capital, higher carried interest beyond certain thresholds, and even entrance and exit fees and loads—not that most good funds charge these, but we have seen them.

The issue with Option 4 is getting access to the good venture capital funds. A really top-tier venture capital firm does not want individuals as limited partners, unless you know the general partners, bring exceptional capabilities and assets, or have unprecedented access to deals, investors, acquirers, or some combination thereof. If you are one of the very small group of people that a top-tier venture capital firm will allow to invest in its funds, it can be a great move to do so. It may have a high minimum (often $1M or more), so this is not an easy option for most accredited investors but worth considering.

If you don't have that access, we would recommend you avoid this option altogether. Most venture capital firms outside the top quartile will not create economic value for you as noted above. Most remaining ways to play this option are either by giving capital to a top-tier venture capitalist who is creating their own first-time fund or by investing in a fund of funds. In the former, the venture capitalists raising a new fund will often take individuals because they need all the capital they can raise. Again, you probably need to know them to find them, and remember to do exhaustive due diligence on them. The reality is that many people you will meet who are leaving established firms are doing so because they are considered to be unsuccessful in that firm. So, why should you be backing them? There are diamonds in the rough, but a lot of work will be needed to validate the story they tell.

The latter option is to invest in a fund of funds. Many large banks and brokerage firms may offer these types of funds. Essentially, they pool your and other investor money into a fund that then goes out and invests as a limited partner into other venture capital funds. If the fund of funds has great access to top-tier venture capital firms, this can appear attractive, although your returns will be reduced by the fund of funds costs—typically in addition to the 2% and 20% or 2.5% and 25% that the venture capital funds will charge, the fund of funds will add another 1% and 10% or in some cases a substantial upfront load of some percentage points. These fees on fees put a real brake on the resulting returns that you will earn. The other major issue with venture capital fund of funds is that most only have a few very good funds in their portfolio—and may add other less attractive funds to which they have greater access. You need to explore this very carefully in your due diligence and make sure you know not only which funds are going to be in the portfolio you are investing into but also what percentage of the fund of funds is made up of those top-tier names that will be very visible in the marketing materials.

One other variant of this strategy that we should also briefly cover is being a passive investor in secondary market positions being sold by current investors. In the past, emerging growth company equity might be available if a founder or employee needed to sell some in order to fund other needs, including taxes. These positions may be offered to investors who are willing to take on the risk of the investment and will pay a valuation close to the most recently completed round valuation. Today, some venture investors also seek to liquidate portions of their holdings by offering some of their investment position on the secondary market, including through portals like Sharespost. Whether offered by founders, employees, or investors, these secondary market opportunities may be directly in the stock of the company itself (you appear on the shareholder list), or they may be in special purpose vehicles (SPVs) that someone has created to allow investors in without having to get the approval of the company because, in many cases, the company has a first right of refusal or can even block a sale of stock to a third party investor. SPVs will often have costs associated with them that need to be understood since they will reduce your potential return.

Secondary market investment opportunities are most frequently available in the best-known unicorns, which are valued at many billions of dollars. Critical issues for an investor include knowing which form of security you will be buying (common stock, preferred stock, etc.), determining the valuation per share of the most recent fundraising transactions of the company, and knowing what rights exist further up the investment waterfall than the investment you are making. Without going into too much detail, we are seeing later-stage investors asking for terms and conditions, which can make it less likely that investors in prior rounds will earn the return they might otherwise have expected. Since most founders and employees will offer you common stock, this is an analysis that is critical to make, but the information is very hard to acquire.

In summary, being a passive investor in a venture capital fund can be attractive if you can gain access to a top-tier fund and if you can afford the minimum commitment required. However, for most readers this is an unlikely option. Meanwhile, being a secondary market investor requires a great deal of financial analysis capability and access to information that may be hard to come by.

This is a good option for you if your scorecard was checked:

1. Rely on Advisors (or maybe First Mover or Fast Follower but see 2)
2. Investor (Passive)
3. Personal Capital and Risk Tolerance. The rest helps if it gets you access.

Having explained that the two venture capital fund options are not very likely for most readers, we can now share the good news: there are three options that are open to almost anyone who wants to play. These three options are being an active angel investor (Option 5), being a passive investor in angel co-investment funds (Option 6), or being a crowdfunding investor (Option 7).

Back in 1997, we had begun to make a few angel investments in the run-up to the dotcom boom and bust. At the time, we were both full-time consulting partners at AT Kearney, but entrepreneurs were beginning to approach us for funding and we had capital to invest. As the years went by, we saw our small portfolio beginning to include some winners, so in 2000 after leaving Gap where Matthew had been SVP global strategy and business development, we explored full-time angel investing but quickly found you can't be an angel by yourself. This is a team game. You need access to a broader funnel of opportunities, you need to do due diligence and negotiate your terms and conditions in a group, and it takes a whole band of angels to bring all the ongoing support an early-stage company needs to begin to get traction. So, we put that on hold until 2006 when we again became full-time angel investors and members of Band of Angels and Keiretsu Forum. The next three options summarize what we have learned and what we believe as regards the opportunity for our readers to build their fortunes by becoming angel investors or exploring the new field of crowdfunding.

Option 5. Active Investor: Angel Investor

Unlike venture capitalists, angel investors are individuals who invest their own capital in the companies they back. Typically, although not always, angel investors are active investors, which is to say that they actively search out good opportunities, conduct deep and expert-based due diligence with other like-minded angels, negotiate their terms and conditions, and then once invested in the company, they actively assist the founders and management with ongoing issues, such as setting strategy, raising additional funding, fine-tuning products and services, going to market, improving operations, expanding markets, including internationally, and so forth. Angel investors often take seats on the board of directors or advisory boards of the companies they invest in, and they often bring substantial expertise to bear.

Because angel investors are investing their own money, they tend to do so in companies that are close to home, both geographically close to home and also in industries and sectors that the angel has prior experience and expertise in. Most angel investors will fall into one of four types:

- The first type of angel is a successful entrepreneur. They will have been entrepreneurs earlier in their careers, and with the capital resulting from their own successful exit(s) they will now be looking for other entrepreneurs to back and help. A good example is our friend Kevin Hartz, who was educated at Stanford and Oxford and began his career at Silicon Graphics. Becoming a technology entrepreneur, Kevin was the founder or co-founder of Eventbrite, ConnectGroup, and Xoom (the first and last being unicorns of the first degree). Kevin transitioned to being a prolific angel investor and backed a number of important companies, including Airbnb, Lookout, PayPal, Pinterest, Skybox Imaging, Trulia, Uber, and Yammer. Today Kevin has joined Founder's Fund as a venture capital general partner.

- The second type of angel is a corporate or services professional. After a successful career leading large companies, becoming a law, accounting, banking, consulting, public relations, or other professional partner, or building expertise and capital by providing other forms of corporate services, many professionals decide to use their expertise and capital to help start-ups to be successful. While rarely successful entrepreneurs themselves, these angels have leverageable and important capabilities, relationships, and other assets to bring to the table. At Keiretsu Forum there are several hundred such angels, some of whom are retired from their corporate and professional lives, while many continue to hold those positions and practice angel investing as a part-time hobby. One example is good friend James Zhang. James has spent his career leading Concept Art House, which provides art and services to leading digital entertainment companies, both videogame and film. James has now leveraged his position in these industries to become a successful angel in areas like digital content, AR, and VR.

- The third type of angel is a full-time investor in another asset class. Often venture capitalists, private equity general partners, hedge fund managers, real-estate investors, and other asset class investors who have substantial capital under management and great personal wealth decide to be angels in their spare time, as a hobby and a way to gain exposure to an asset class that is not their day job. Randy Williams, who founded Keiretsu, is a very good example of an angel who first was a successful investor in another asset class: in Randy's case, real estate. After attending UC Berkeley and St. Mary's College, Randy began his career in real estate as a commercial broker. By 2000, Randy had benefited greatly from successful real-estate transactions and wanted to diversify into the early-stage technology asset class. Knowing that this was not his area of expertise, he gathered his friends together, many of whom were also leading real-estate investors, and formed an investment club in Lafayette, California, which became the first chapter of Keiretsu Forum, which is today the world's leading angel network (see Sidebar 1: Keiretsu Forum and Keiretsu Capital).

- The fourth type of angel is everyone else. This can include people with inherited wealth, those just entering the ranks of accredited investor, and increasingly it also includes current technology entrepreneurs who are looking to back a small group of companies beyond the one that they spend every day running.

When we talk to angels like Kevin, James, and Randy, and ask them why they choose to invest their time and capital into backing technology entrepreneurs, a number of answers always come up. First, that there is a belief that the future will be driven by disruptive technologies and a desire to participate in changing the world. Second, there is a keen understanding that the angel asset class is one of the highest returning in the world, if enough companies are in your portfolio. Third, most angels talk about their desire to mentor and coach others, and bring their own expertise, experience, and relationships to bear in helping technology entrepreneurs. Additionally, we always hear angels say that they find the disruptive innovations, technologies, and business models being developed by the early-stage companies as being a source of enormous fascination and learning. Most angels like to be immersed in the future through the lens of the entrepreneurs and the companies that they back. Finally, many angels are looking to their own legacies and the impact that their investing can have on improving the future for their own children and families. As one angel told us as we prepared to write this book, "I wonder what my legacy will be—transforming the world, now that sounds like a worthy one."

Professor Jeffrey Sohl at the University of New Hampshire tracks new business formation in the US that is backed by angel investors. According to his annual research, in 2016:

- 71,110 businesses (in contrast with the 7,750 backed by VCs in 2016) were backed by angel investors.
- In each of the last 3 years, angels exceeded $24 billion in funding (2015 – $24.6 billion, 2014 – $24.1 billion, and 2013 – $24.8 billion).
- 304,930 angels were active in backing these businesses.
- Most of these businesses were technology start-ups: 18% were in software, 16% in healthcare, 13% in biotech, 11% in industrial and energy, and 9% in new media.
- In addition, other sectors backed by angels, such as retail (11%), also include many technology-enabled businesses.

When analyzed by round of investment, angels are backing true start-ups in their formation as well as in their seed and sometimes Series A rounds. Conversely, very few angels follow-on invest into the subsequent rounds (Series B and beyond).

Do angels get good returns? Most academic research that has been conducted into the activities of angels finds that they do very well, as demonstrated in Sidebar 5: The Expected Returns of Angel Investors in Groups, in Part 2 of this book. Their returns are among the best of any asset class, consistently in the mid-20%s annual returns, according to most researchers.

If angels investing in groups get attractive returns, how do they do so? By being disciplined and ensuring they behave consistently across their angel investing activities, angels investing in groups appear to raise the probability of achieving an attractive return. Professor Robert Wiltbank shows that angel returns appear to be correlated with:

- **Due Diligence Focus.** Conducting significant hours of collaborative, expert-based due diligence drives returns. 65% of the exits with below-median due diligence reported less than 1x returns, whereas when angels spent more than 40 hours doing due diligence, they experienced a 7.1x multiple.
- **Industry Expertise.** Angels earned returns twice as high for investments in ventures connected to their own industry expertise, and many of their best exits came in this way.
- **Interaction with Portfolio Companies.** Angels who interacted with the venture a couple of times a month after making their investment experienced a 3.7x multiple in 4 years, whereas investors who participated a couple of times a year experienced multiples of only 1.3x in 3.6 years.

Investors wishing to achieve the attractive returns of angel investing would be wise to join and be active in angel groups that share these three characteristics in their organizational cultures.

These behaviors are in marked contrast to organizations that may do little due diligence or external professional due diligence, that may be led by investors who themselves do not have expertise in the industries of the portfolio companies, and/or that may focus on being passive after the investment is made, rather than at the extreme of active investing.

We agree with the view that not everyone should choose to be an angel investor. Conversely, we believe every one of the 12.5 million American households that qualify as accredited could choose to be angels—we all have something valuable to offer to some worthy entrepreneur.

Pros and Cons

So, choosing to be an active angel investor can pay off. Very handsomely. But, you need to have the capabilities and assets to play the game. You need to be diligent, hardworking in support of your companies, and you need the capital, relationships, time, and risk tolerance needed to participate. There are already 300,000 or more US angel investors, so it is not that hard to get started: the barriers to entry are quite low.

You must be diversified across a lot of deals. Otherwise, you expose yourself to the risk of total capital loss. We recommend that an angel investor build a portfolio of around 40 deals in order to achieve proper diversification. This is challenging, and most angels fail to do this (Sidebar 7: Capturing the Angel Returns).

This is a good option for you if your scorecard was checked:

1. Fast Follower (or maybe First Mover)
2. Innovator, Entrepreneur, or Investor (Active)
3. Most of the leverageable asset boxes, and if you checked Corporate, maybe you can be an Institutional Angel Investor.

As an angel investor, you are no different from the venture capitalists except you have to make do with your own capital and adjust your strategies accordingly. You get to sit at home and know your investments just might change the world—and, really, what could beat that feeling?

Sidebar 7: Capturing the Angel Returns

In 2015 we asked more than 250 angel investors, who are members of Keiretsu Forum in the US and Canada, questions to assess what they had learned from the academic research in terms of the likely returns and the number of investments they would need to make in order to have a high likelihood of capturing those returns. Our findings were:

Realistic Expectations. Angels have realistic and perhaps slightly low expectations for the return they expect from investing in their angel group. While the academic research suggests returns as high as 27% IRR, the angels surveyed were split between a group of 113 investors (45%) expecting returns between 10% to 20% and 140 investors (55%) expecting returns above 20%.

Need for Diversification Understood. Angels understand the need for diversification. The angels surveyed were split between a group of 106 investors (42%) who thought 15 to 30 investments sufficient and 144 investors (57%) who believed more than 30 investments would be necessary. Three investors thought that a portfolio of less than 15 deals would achieve diversification. Almost all of the angels surveyed believed that diversification would be beneficial towards raising the probability of getting the angel return.

Almost No Angels Achieve Diversification. Conversely, while understanding what diversification implies, almost no angels surveyed had a large enough portfolio to have a statistically high likelihood of achieving the angel return. The vast majority of the angels reported that they had fewer than 15 angel deals in their personal portfolios (206 investors or 81%). A group of 43 angel investors, or 17%, have between 15 and 30 investments. And only 4, or 2%, had more than 30 deals in their personal portfolios of angel-backed companies.

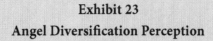

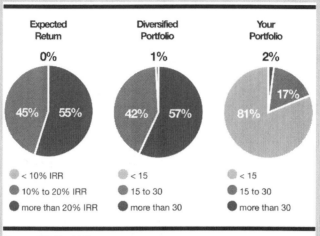

Exhibit 23
Angel Diversification Perception

Source: Fifth Era, LLC

Comparing these findings, it is striking to see that while 99% of angels believe that they need portfolios of more than 15 investments, only 19% of angel investors accomplished this level of diversification.

Given these findings, we then asked the angels the open-ended question, "Why are you undiversified, given that you understand the attractiveness of the expected angel return and the number of deals required to have a high likelihood of achieving it?"

The most common reasons given were along the following lines:

"My net worth will not allow me to invest in enough deals. Since most companies have a $50,000 or $25,000 minimum investment size for a direct angel investment, I would need to dedicate too much into angel deals to build the portfolio size needed for diversification. I have a maximum of 10% of my net worth available for these types of investments."

"I believe in the thesis that I need to do many hours of due diligence and many hours of active participation in each deal. I can't support a large number of companies as an active angel investor—5 to 10 is about all I can cope with given the personal time commitments."

"Even being active in Keiretsu Forum, I don't attend enough meetings to see enough deals that I would like to invest in, and certainly not 7 to 10 per year. I have a full-time job, and with vacations and other commitments I may be attending 6 or 7 times a year and investing 2 or 3 times a year."

"I am uncomfortable investing outside my own area of expertise even though I know other members in the room do have that deep industry knowledge. And within my own area of expertise I don't see enough good deals a year."

"I am based in city xxxxxxx, and that is where I see most of my deals. I don't see that many here each year that I want to invest in. If someone would show me deals in other cities that met my criteria and also which I could trust had been the subject of the discipline I expect when investing, then perhaps that would be a solution."

In short, the angel investors surveyed for the most part had realistic expectations regarding the angel return, understood the need for diversification given the skewed nature of returns, and had a reasonable sense of what diversification implied in terms of portfolio count. But, because of practical considerations, they were unable to get there in terms of making enough investments in their own portfolios.

This provides clarity to perhaps the most important challenge facing angels investing in groups. Given their capital constraints, their need to diversify, and their desire to benefit from the angel return, they need to make many more smaller investments in angel-backed technology companies.

Source: Le Merle, M., & Le Merle, L. (2015). Capturing the expected returns of angel investors in groups—Less in more, diversify. Fifth Era LLC.

Option 6. Passive Investor: Angel Co-Investment Funds

This is a relatively new option. Some angel groups have created co-investment vehicles that invest in all or some of the companies that their angel groups back. At Band of Angels where we have been members for a decade, Ian Sobieski, who is the president, is also general partner of the Acorn Fund, which selectively backs companies that his angel members are investing in. So too at Angels' Forum where the founder, Carol Sands, is also the lead partner in the Halo Funds. At Keiretsu Forum, we have created a whole family of such funds within Keiretsu Capital, including funds that invest in the same rounds as the angels, a venture fund that follows on in the first institutional venture capital round, and a real-estate fund to give members access to a diversified real-estate fund portfolio.

Most of these angel co-investment funds are intended to solve the diversification challenge for the active angel members of the group, as well as help them invest in areas they may be uncomfortable directly investing in or in deals that they may have otherwise missed. At Keiretsu Capital, our funds each invest in more than 40 companies so that if our angels have backed perhaps 10 or 15 companies directly, they can supplement their portfolio with another 40 through each fund they invest in.

A handful of these angel co-investment funds may be open to investors, who are not members of the angel group and who are not active angel investors. This provides a powerful opportunity to people who would otherwise not have access to disruptive technology companies being backed by the leading angel investors. In our funds we have investors from Europe and Asia who are investing specifically because they want some of their capital to go into US technology companies in the early stage of funding, but they would not otherwise be able to make investments in these companies.

Since Keiretsu Forum is the most active venture investor by number of deals in the US (more than 160 companies backed in 2016), the network provides a powerful deal-flow funnel for the co-investment funds to use to create portfolios of diversified Fifth Era emerging technology companies. Even more so, Keiretsu, because of its position as the largest angel group, also sees great deals syndicated to it from other leading angel groups (and vice versa). So, even more opportunities enter the funnel each cycle.

Pros and Cons

Angel co-investment funds allow passive investors (or active) to put capital to work across large portfolios of Fifth Era companies that other active angel investors have backed with their own capital. This is the purest economic signal since you are committing capital only after experienced angel investors have completed all of their due diligence, made the decision to invest their own capital, and the round is close to closing.

The major disadvantages are similar to the venture capital fund disadvantages. Funds charge fees, and your returns are reduced as a result. If you could have been a direct and active angel investor, investing your capital without fees directly into the companies a large number of times, then you would have a higher return at the end of the day than by investing through an angel co-investment fund.

Again, watch out for the small print. Angel co-investment funds are new, and they don't all operate in the way described here. Be sure you read the small print and you understand where the vested interests lie (who will make money off your money) and that the fund will operate in the way you want it to operate for what will be probably be a decade, and maybe more.

This is a good option for you if your scorecard was checked:

1. Rely on Advisors (or maybe First Mover or Fast Follower but see 2)
2. Investor (Passive)
3. Personal Capital and Risk Tolerance. Access will not be an issue here.

Option 7. Crowdfunding Investor

Over the last few years, the US has worked towards making it easier for the broader population to invest in small businesses in order to democratize start-up investing beyond organized VC funds and accredited angel investors. This has seen the passing of the "Jumpstart Our Business Start-ups Act" or JOBS Act. First signed into law by President Obama in 2012, the act continues to be made into law as the SEC reviews and releases additional components of regulation. The JOBS Act as originally passed would, among other things, do the following:

- Allow for an increase in the number of shareholders a company may have before being required to register its common stock with the SEC and become a publicly reporting company.
- Provide an exemption from the need to register public offerings with the SEC that would allow the use of Internet funding portals, including "equity crowdfunding platforms" (with certain limits on how much an investor can invest through these portals).
- Create a new definition of "emerging-growth companies" as those with less than $1 billion in revenues.
- Relieve these companies from some regulatory and disclosure requirements when they go public.
- Lift the ban on "general solicitation" and advertising of specific kinds of private placements.

The JOBS Act has stimulated the formation of a very large number of "equity crowdfunding" platforms and businesses. While the potential may be significant in terms of providing additional avenues for start-ups to receive funding, the current progress is modest. Crowdnetic, which tracks the major crowdfunding platforms in the US, reports that from September 23, 2013 through September 23, 2015 (two years):

- There were 6,063 distinct offerings, of which 1,596 were successful in raising commitments of $870 million for an average of $545,122 per successful issuer.
- California alone accounted for 472 of the successful offerings raising $270 million.
- The top three sectors benefitting were real-estate development, real-estate investment, and oil and gas production and pipelines—thus, technology start-ups were not the leading recipients of equity crowdfunding in that time period.
- The two real-estate sectors accounted for $208.3 million of the $870 million (23.9%) in total commitments made

through equity crowdfunding platforms tracked by Crowd-netic.

So, while crowdfunding shows promise in terms of being a viable approach to backing start-ups, in practice the $870 million raised to date has seen a majority invested outside technology start-ups. Furthermore, that $870 million pales in comparison to the more than $69 billion the VCs invest primarily in later-stage rounds and the $24.6 billion that the angels invest primarily in formation through Series A rounds.

However, crowdfunding might be a good way for you to dip a toe into being an investor in early-stage technology companies. The advantages are that you can make very small investments, don't need to do your own extensive due diligence, and can, as a result, build a large diversified portfolio quickly. Perhaps the leading equity crowdfunding platform in the US is AngelList founded by Nadal Ravikant in 2010. Today AngelList is backed by a number of venture investors, including CSC Group of China, which makes additional capital available to deals that have been taken through the crowdfunding process. Among the syndicate managers who are most active on AngelList is Gil Penchina, one of the early executives at eBay and a prolific investor.

The disadvantages are that crowdfunding is new and we do not yet know the returns or failure rates for the types of deals appearing on the platforms. It will likely be another 5 or 10 years before that becomes clear. Additionally, you don't know exactly what due diligence has been done and by whom. In some cases the syndicate managers who are putting forward investment opportunities may not have your interests at heart: they get compensated by sharing any returns you make, so in some cases they may care more about getting you to invest than about the risk-adjusted return that you will experience. So, as with all investing, you need to do your own due diligence, uncover other people's motivations and vested interests, and only invest when you are sure you know the lay of the land.

This is a good option for you if your scorecard was checked:

1. Rely on Advisors
2. Investor (Passive)
3. Personal Capital and Risk Tolerance. Access will not be an issue here.

Before we describe the final two options for building your fortune in the Fifth Era, let's go back in time and take a look at a strategy used in the Great California Gold Rush.

In 1849, California experienced its famous Gold Rush. During this year and the next few, hundreds of thousands of people from around the world came to San Francisco to head for the hills and make their own fortunes. Early the year before, in 1848, employees of John Sutter who owned land near Coloma, California, began to appear in the store of Samuel Brannan at Sutter's Fort. They wanted to pay for their goods with gold that they had found in the rivers around the area.

Sam Brannan suddenly realized he was ideally situated: he operated the only store between San Francisco and the gold fields that sold the items that every budding gold miner needed. Brannan bought more tools, equipment, and supplies, and kept on selling at ever-inflated prices as more and more miners began to move into the mountains and goldfields. Brannan used his profits (and perhaps some of the tithes from his parishioners at the Church of Latter Day Saints) to buy up land in San Francisco, Sacramento, and eventually as far afield as Hawaii and Southern California. Sam Brannan became California's first millionaire and shortly afterward was elected California State Senator.

Perhaps, you can be the next Sam Brannan. The next two options are updated versions of what Sam Brannan was doing back in 1849.

Option 8. Provider of an Incubator and/or Accelerator

Due to the emergence of digital technologies, an increasing number of people have felt able to start entrepreneurial ventures. On the one hand, the costs of doing so have greatly reduced, and on the other hand, the twin forces of globalization and digitalization have expanded addressable markets to the point that start-ups are able to serve customers globally almost from the day they are founded. It has never been easier to launch a new technology-enabled company.

However, with VCs investing later and angel groups selective about the number of formation-phase start-up firms led by first-time founders that they choose to become involved with, there has been a gap in the funding environment for start-ups. First-time founders need some capital, but much more importantly they need a great deal of education, mentorship, and access to capabilities for their start-up. And they need a base location, too.

In the days of the gold rush, people like Sam Brannan stepped up, providing board and lodging for gold miners at very high prices and making sure that they received the essential information about how to use the gold rush equipment (pans, sluices, sorters and so on) at the same time as they were sold for the highest price the miner could afford. Today's equivalent is that technology entrepreneurs want their own place to begin their ventures and they need early coaching and mentoring especially if they are first time entrepreneurs.

While some angel groups provide such resources, the great demand across the US from first-time founders has led to new models in which some combination of a place to base the company, an environment of support and mentorship, and perhaps a little funding allow for a higher likelihood of moving past the first six months of entrepreneurial-formation activities.

Incubators and accelerators have become this alternative for many first-time CEOs. While somewhat simplified, the distinction between incubators and accelerators is that incubators generally have a non-competitive selection process and focus on formation- to seed-stage companies. Conversely, most accelerators have a highly competitive selection process, are generally centered around an investment business model, last 3 to 6 months, and have intense mentorship programs on-site. There are many alternative models within this new and emerging field; however, some dimensions across which they vary include:

- They may have a physical space, or they may be virtual in nature. Some focus on providing office space only while others focus on the acceleration activities.

- Some charge a monthly or weekly fee for space—perhaps $600 for a desk with access to shared facilities—but do not take equity. This is the "real-estate incubator model" as used at WeWork, founded by Adam Neuman in New York in 2010 that we mentioned earlier in the book, and RocketSpace, founded by Duncan Logan in San Francisco in 2011.

- Others take equity (often in the 5% to 10% range) and may provide a small cash grant (typically between $25,000 and $50,000). This is the "equity-based accelerator model" as practiced by 500 Startups, TechStars and YCombinator, for example.

- Some may have follow-on funds that can invest in the seed or even Series A rounds of those companies that they see getting the most traction though most start-ups in incubators and accelerators do not move into these phases.

- Additionally, some provide "access to innovation" services for corporate sponsors who want to "scout" the innovation ecosystem and perhaps discover companies for subsequent partnerships.

Angel investors are an important component in this entrepreneurial ecosystem and are actively involved as mentors and advisors for incubator and accelerator programs alike. In many cases, accelerator managers are also active angel investors who provide additional financing to some of the ventures, either directly or via a fund. In this way, incubators and accelerators work symbiotically with angels who are often actively involved in visiting the nascent start-ups and provide both financial and advisory support. All have active and vested interest in helping these start-ups flourish.

First-time CEOs need to be clear on what they are looking for before they begin to pitch to incubators and accelerators given this wide diversity of offerings. And, they should be very careful about sharing equity unless they are sure they cannot source similar support from their initial friends, family, and angel investors—often for free. However, for many first-time CEOs, this is a valuable new source of support in the early stages of life.

There is very little quantitative data regarding the funding of startups by incubators and accelerators. Based on a new study conducted by the Brookings Institution Metropolitan Policy Program (2016):

- Accelerators have experienced rapid growth in recent years in the US, increasing more than tenfold from just 16 programs in 2008 to 170 programs in 2014.
- The 172 accelerators tracked by the study supported 5,259 companies over ten years, or an average of 525 companies a year (compared to 71,110 backed by angels in 2015).
- The accelerators themselves provided $2.6 billion over ten years to the companies or an average of $260 million per year (compared to $24.1 billion provided by the angels in 2014).
- While the annual capital made available has been growing as some accelerators, like Y-Combinator and 500 Startups, raise follow-on funds, it is still believed to be less than $500 million a year in aggregate (excluding the capital provided by angels and VCs to companies graduating from the programs).

So, while incubators and accelerators play an important role in the ecosystem, and some, such as Y-Combinator, Rocketspace, and 500 Startups, have become viable sources of capital, for the most part startups receive their capital in the seed round from the angel investors who engage with the companies emerging from the incubators and accelerators.

Operating an incubator and/or accelerator is clearly one option for anyone who wants to create one. To do so you have to be willing to:

- Design your participation strategy—real-estate-related income, equity participation, corporate sponsorship program, etc. What type of incubator and/or accelerator will you be? Will you need space? Will you make investments?
- Lease or otherwise secure a space that can be used if you plan on operating a physical incubator. Some large companies, universities, non-profits, or government entities may be willing to put space at your disposal if your plan is exciting enough.
- If you plan to operate a virtual accelerator, you will still need space for all of your activities even if you don't plan to host the companies yourself.
- Find a source of entrepreneurs and new companies that want flexible workspace and other types of support.
- Build out a curriculum and events, both to make your space more attractive to entrepreneurs and to connect them with others who can make them successful, including the angel investors that they will need to get started.
- Sign up corporate partners and sponsors, both to provide content and also to pay you to scout the ecosystem for companies that have disruptive innovations that they want to secure for their own businesses.
- If you are launching a fund, find limited partners to provide the capital. This may take a while given that you probably need a track record of operating a successful program.
- Work hard to fill up your space and/or programs.
- Work hard to make sure some of your companies are able to raise money at higher valuations so that you can demonstrate your track record of helping companies succeed.

Pros and Cons

Operating an incubator and/or accelerator is something that many people can do even if they are not themselves great innovators, entrepreneurs, or investors. But, it is a lot of hard work to operate a successful incubator and have it always close to occupancy with a steady stream of successful companies leaving to larger spaces with adequate funding.

If you do succeed in doing so, you will have privileged access to a steady flow of new Fifth Era companies. Some believe that because they will be able to cherry pick new start-ups from their captive incubators and accelerators that they should be able to do well, so they are keen to take equity in the companies. Others believe that the failure rate of incubator and accelerator companies is so high that it is better to just take cash from the companies for the space they use and from corporate sponsors who want to get access to the innovations.

Recently, we have seen a few incubator and accelerator funds begin to appear. While typically backed by large institutional investors, some of these new funds also take investor capital from accredited investors. To date there are not enough of these funds with years of operation out there for us to be able to make assessments of how they perform and the returns they achieve. The fund general partners argue that the privileged access argument is real, and they typically point to a list of successful graduates that every incubator and accelerator posts on their walls that have gone on to do great things.

For us, the jury is still out on these new funds, but we encourage you to seek them out and make your own determination.

This is a good option for you if your scorecard was checked:

1. Fast Follower
2. Valuable Service Provider and maybe Investor (Active)
3. Corporate, Relationships, and Time. Maybe Personal Capital and Risk Tolerance, both to start the enterprise and to invest if that is your strategy.

Option 9. Provider of Professional Services to Fifth Era Companies

This option focuses on building a business that works with Fifth Era companies, selling or providing them with whatever they need.

If you are a professional, this may mean selling them the services they need:

- If you are lawyer, you do their formation, fundraising, and follow-on legal work.
- If you are a bookkeeper and/or accountant, you sort out their accounts and finances.
- If you are a fundraiser, you might help them raise money (assuming you have a broker-dealer license).
- If you are a marketer, you help them with branding, strategic planning, market identification, and messaging.
- If you have a high-tech professional services business, maybe you help them sell, distribute, and service their new products.
- And so on.

They need all of these services, just as the gold miners needed their picks, shovels, and pans.

But, they don't have gold to pay you. They probably don't have cash at all. They may have equity, however.

So, in this option, you build a business that leverages your own capabilities and assets, and use it to serve new Fifth Era companies that you select based upon their ability to pay you cash (limited) and the attractiveness of their equity (which you agree to take for the shortfall between what they can pay in cash and what you say your services are worth).

Because you are taking equity, you also hold the risk that the company will fail. So, hopefully you ask for quite a bit more equity than your services would cost in cash (maybe 3 times?), and you are very selective since the failure rate will likely be 50% and more.

And, of course, you "mark up" the value of what you are offering on your side and mark down the value of the equity they want to give you. Value is in the eye of the beholder, and hopefully they need your services greatly, especially before they are funded by angel investors.

One very good example of this option in practice is provided by our good friend Max Shapiro, who has an executive search firm called PeopleConnect. A recovering entrepreneur himself, Max joined Keiretsu Forum as a member in the first chapter that was created in 2000.

He quickly saw that the technology entrepreneurs that come to the angel groups rarely have a complete team: whatever the capabilities and strengths of the founding team, there are always gaps that investors need filled quickly if they are to back the company. Max decided to focus his firm on this opportunity. Though they serve companies of all sizes, PeopleConnect has now established a reputation as specialists in start-up hiring. Most of their clients are innovative start-ups, early-stage ventures, and companies in expansion or turnaround mode, which are building a name in their respective industries. Max has modified the traditional executive search model to specifically address this need and has also been creative in modifying compensation models, including taking equity in some cases.

Another example we are very familiar with is that of Ira Rothken and the Rothken Law Firm. Ira, who is both a lawyer and very technology-savvy investor, has leveraged both together to create a unique firm that understands the pressing issues of the Fifth Era and disruptive technologies and breakthrough innovations, with a deep understanding of technology entrepreneurship and business formation. Taken together, this has made Ira a valuable resource for some of the most innovative companies, including those involved with digital entertainment and ecommerce.

On the more entrepreneurial side, Ira also helped start numerous successful electronic entertainment and videogame companies, including Nihilistic Software, Pandemic Games, Telltale, and Arenanet, and frequently takes equity as partial compensation for his work.

Larger firms also play this game from time to time. At Pillsbury, one of the world's leading law firms, the partners created a special package to enable technology entrepreneurs to launch their companies at a very modest cost with the support that a well-funded company would expect to receive. Pillsbury is not the only firm to do this, although our lawyer there—Riaz Karamali—is a particularly active backer of early-stage companies and an angel investor himself.

Pros and Cons

First and foremost, the advantage of this option is that it allows you to play even if your capital is limited or you are too risk-averse with regard to making cash investments in these companies. You get to trade your own capabilities for cash and equity. Ironically, if you are too risk-averse to be willing to invest your capital, it does seem a little odd that you would be willing to invest your time—time is money, so you should be equally risk-averse with your capital as with your time. However, we do find a lot of people who won't risk their hard-earned capital but are very willing to invest their precious time. Maybe you are one of these people.

Just as Peter Lynch, the famous manager of the Magellan Fund, puts it, "During the Gold Rush, most would-be miners lost money, but people who sold them picks, shovels, tents, and blue-jeans (Levi Strauss) made a nice profit," this can work out very well. Of course, Peter Lynch assumes you can get the new entrepreneurs to pay you cash.

If they pay you with equity, then their failure will be yours too. You are fully aligned—which could be good, but could be bad. The rules of diversification apply here too, just as they do for the cash investors, i.e., venture capitalists and angel investors. You need to create a diversified portfolio of equity positions in these companies to combat the high failure rate. Don't just do this once or twice. Do it tens or scores of times.

Cash is king, so you need to look carefully at your opportunity cost. If you could provide the same services to a large corporation which would pay you handsomely, are you sure that your "services for equity" model will pay off better in the long term?

This is a good option for you if your scorecard was checked:

1. Rely on Advisors
2. Valuable Service Provider and maybe Investor (Passive) or Investor (Active)
3. Time and Risk Tolerance

So, there we are.

Nine distinct options for building your fortune in the Fifth Era. Nine ways to capitalize on how disruptive innovation is generating new wealth-creation opportunities. We promised to get you to this point, and we have.

Chapter 9
Happen to Things

It had long since come to my attention that people of accomplishment rarely sat back and let things happen to them. They went out and happened to things.

—Leonardo Da Vinci

For 30, years we have been in Silicon Valley and have been exposed to the world's leading innovation cluster. Over that time, almost by osmosis, we have observed and absorbed from others so much about this most dynamic of times. This book summarizes what we have learned. To reiterate:

- The world is entering a new era: the Fifth Era.
- This is being driven by a host of disruptive innovations, with the Digital Revolution and the Biotechnology Revolution central among them.
- Everything we as humans do is being questioned at the most fundamental of levels.
- The underlying assumptions, formulated in the Industrial Era and in the eras before it, around which we've structured our lives, cannot be taken for granted.
- Each time new disruptive technologies enable an underlying assumption to be made obsolete, they open up the way for new business opportunities—and for the entrepreneurs and businesses that exploit them.
- This represents the greatest wealth-creation opportunity the world has ever seen.
- Wealth is being captured earlier than in the past by the entrepreneurs themselves and by those that back them.
- Most people are on the sidelines. Only 0.2% of the US working

population are becoming fundable technology entrepreneurs each year, and only 2.5% of the accredited investor households are investing as venture capitalists or angel investors.

- Meanwhile, the principal investment strategy of the Industrial Era of investing in the public markets does not seem to work as well anymore.

- Instead, in this time of transition you need to invest early in disruptive technology companies in order to secure your position or find another option for playing and building your fortune in the Fifth Era.

If you have followed and agreed with our thesis to this point, then the good news is that there are a lot of ways to play:

- First, take stock of yourself: your objectives, who you are or could be, and the capabilities and assets that you bring with you.

- Then, review the nine options and determine which handful best suits your circumstance.

- There is an option for everyone.

Now is the time for action. The time of transition is not only one through which the world is passing, but also it is a time of transition for many people. The coming Fifth Era is a chance for each person to make a choice to change from being a spectator on the sidelines to an active player in the greatest of games.

And, for those of our readers who decide to go another way and take a purposeful decision not to participate, we would like to end by sharing with them a final thought:

One day you might wake up and realize that you slept through the greatest moment of change the world has ever seen. We implore you to not let that happen to you.

Good luck.

It's the job that's never started as takes longest to finish.
—J. R. R. Tolkien

References

Aguila-Obra, A., Padilla-Melendez, A., and Serarols-Tarres, C. (2007). Value creation and new intermediaries on Internet. An exploratory analysis of the online news industry and the web content aggregators. *International Journal of Information Management, 27*(3), 187–199.

Andrews, E. (2017). Is tech disruption good for the economy? Retrieved from https://www.gsb.stanford.edu/insights/tech-disruption-good-economy

Angel Resource Institute at Willamette University. (2015). Halo report—2015 annual report. Retrieved from https://angelresourceinstitute.org/reports/halo-report-full-version-ye-2015.pdf

A.T. Kearney Global Management Consulting Company (2015). *Connected risks: Investing in a divergent world. The 2015 A.T. Kearney Foreign Direct Investment Confidence Index.* Retrieved from https://www.atkearney.com/documents/10192/5797358/Connected+Risks%E2%80%94Investing+in+a+Divergent+World.pdf/e45b9ffa-700b-445e-bb34-e2dfff082009

Atkinson, R. D., Ezell, S. J., Andes, S. M., Castro, D. D., & Bennett, R. (2010). The Internet economy 25 years after .com: Transforming commerce and life. The Information Technology and Innovative Foundation. Retrieved from http://www.itif.org/files/2010-25-years.pdf

Bank of Montreal Wealth Institute (2015). Women in wealth: A financial golden age has arrived. Retrieved from https://www.bmo.com/pdf/ewp/womeninwealth/15-375-BWI_Q1_2015-women-in-wealth-CDN-E05web.pdf

Barton, D., Chen, Y., & Jin, A. (2013). Mapping China's middle class. Retrieved from http://www.mckinsey.com/industries/retail/our-insights/mapping-chinas-middle-class

Beardsley, B., Holley, B., Jaafar, M., Muxi, F., Neumann, M., Tang, T., . . . Zakrzewski, A. (2016). Global wealth 2016: Navigating the new client landscape. Retrieved from https://www.bcgperspectives.com/content/articles/financial-institutions-consumer-insight-global-wealth-2016/

Bilbao-Osorio, B., Dutta, S., & Lanvin, B. (Eds.). (2014). The global information technology report 2014: The rewards and risks of big data. (1st ed.). Geneva: World Economic Forum and INSEAD. Retrieved from http://www3.weforum.org/docs/WEF_GlobalInformationTechnology_Report_2014.pdf

Brookings (2016). *Accelerating growth: Startup accelerator programs in the United States.* Washington, DC: Hathaway, I. Retrieved from https://www.brookings.edu/research/accelerating-growth-startup-accelerator-programs-in-the-united-states/

Central Intelligence Agency. (2016). The world factbook. Retrieved fromnhttps://www.cia.gov/library/publications/the-world-factbook/geos/xx.html

Childe, G. V. (1929). *The most ancient east: The oriental prelude to European prehistory.* New York, NY: Alfred A. Knopf.

Crowdnetic. (2015). Crowdnetic's quarterly private companies publicly raising data analysis. Title II turns two. Retrieved from http://www.crowdnetic.com/reports/sep-2015-report

Cumming, D., & John, S. (2014). The economic impact of entrepreneurship: Comparing international datasets. *Corporate Governance: An International Review, 22,* 162–178.

Dean, D., Digrande, S., Field, D., Lundmark, A., O'Day, J., . . . Zwillenberg, P. (2012). Connected world series: The Internet economy in the G-20: The $4.2 trillion growth opportunity. The Boston Consulting Group. Retrieved from https://www.bcg.com/documents/file100409.pdf

DeGennaro, R., & Dwyer, G. (2010). Expected returns to stock investments by angel investors in groups. Retrieved from https://www.frbatlanta.org/research/publications/wp/2010/14.aspx

Deloitte LLP (2014). Foreign direct investment and inclusive growth: The impacts on social progress. Retrieved from https://www2.deloitte.com/content/dam/Deloitte/global/Documents/About-Deloitte/gx-dttl-FDI-and-inclusive-growth.pdf

De Treville, S., Petty, J., & Wager, S. (2014). Economies of extremes: Lessons from venture-capital decision making. *Journal of Operations Management, 32*(6). doi: 10.1016/j.jom.2014.07.002

Dietz, L. D. (1997). The legal and regulatory environment of the Internet. *Information Systems Security, 6*(1), 55–63.

Dogsofthedow (2017). [table listing 50 largest companies by market capitalization available on major U.S. stock exchanges]. Largest companies by market cap today. Retrieved from http://dogsofthedow.com/largest-companies-by-market-cap.htm

Dow Jones VentureSource (2016). Venture capital report, U.S. 4Q 2015. Dow Jones. Retrieved from http://images.dowjones.com/wp-content/uploads/sites/43/2016/01/21024130/DJ-VentureSource-US_4Q15-.pdf

Ernst & Young (2014). Adapting and evolving: Global venture capital insights and trends 2014. Retrieved from http://www.ey.com/Publication/vwLUAssets/Global_venture_capital_insights_and_trends_2014/$FILE/EY_Global_VC_insights_and_trends_report_2014.pdf

European Commission Joint Research Centre Institute for Prospective Technological Studies (2010). *The 2010 report on R&D and ICT in the European Union 2010.* Luxembourg: Turlea, G., Nepelski, D., de Prato, G., Lindmark, S., de Panizza, A., Picci, L., . . . Broster, D.

Farhadi, M., Ismail, R., & Fooladi, M. (2012). Information and communication technology use and economic growth. *PLoS ONE, 7*(11), e48903. doi:10.1371/journal.pone.0048903

Faria, A., & Barbosa, N. (2014). Does venture capital really foster innovation? *Economics Letters, 122* (2), 129–131.

Forbes (2009, February 19). Top 30 innovations of the last 30 years. Retrieved from https://www.forbes.com/2009/02/19/innovation-internet-health-entrepreneurs-technology_wharton.html

Friedrich, R., Peterson, M., Koster, A., & Blum, S. (2010). The rise of generation C—Implications for the world of 2020. Booz & Company. Retrieved from http://www.strategyand.pwc.com/media/file/Strategyand_Rise-of-Generation-C.pdf.pdf

Friedrich, R., Le Merle, M., Peterson, M., & Koster, A. (2011). The next wave of digitization—Setting your direction, building your capabilities. Booz & Company. Retrieved from http://www.strategyand.pwc.com/media/uploads/Strategyand-Next-Wave-of-Digitization.pdf

Friedrich, R., Peterson, M., Koster, A., Grone, F. & Le Merle, M. (2011). Measuring industry digitization—Leaders and laggards in the digital economy. Booz & Company. Retrieved from http://www.strategyand.pwc.com/reports/measuring-industry-digitization-leaders-laggards

George, L., & Hogendorn, C. (2012). Aggregators, search and the economics of new media institutions. *Information Economics and Policy, 24*(1): 40–51.

Georgiades, E. (2010). Copyright liability for users and distributors of content sharing and communication technologies: A crossroads between past and present. *Information & Communications Technology Law, 19*(1), 1–26. http://dx.doi.org/10.1080/13600831003593154

Glover, T. (2012, March 3). Middle East angel investors daring to turn their sights homeward. *The National.* Retrieved from http://www.

thenational.ae/lifestyle/personal-finance/middle-east-angel-investors-daring-to-turn-their-sights-homeward

Grilli, L., & Murtinu, S. (2014). Government, venture capital and the growth of European high-tech entrepreneurial firms. *Research Policy, 43*(9), 1523–1543.

GSMA (2014). The mobile economy 2014. London: U.K. Retrieved from https://www.gsmaintelligence.com/research/?file=bb688b-369d64cfd5b4e05a1ccfcbcb48&download

Hobbes, T. (1651). *Leviathan.*

Ibrahim, D. (2010). Financing the next Silicon Valley. *Washington University Law Review, 87*(4), 717–762.

Kende, M. (2014). Global Internet report 2014. Geneva: Internet Society. Retrieved from https://www.internetsociety.org/sites/default/files/Global_Internet_Report_2014.pdf

Kogan, L., Papanikolaou, D., Seru. A., & Stoffman, N. (2012). Technological innovation, resource allocation, and growth. National Bureau of Economic Research (NBER). doi: 10.3386/w17769

Kuhn, T. (1962). *The structure of scientific revolutions.* Chicago, IL: University of Chicago Press.

Kunstner, T., Le Merle, M., Gmelin, H., & Dietsche, C. (2013). The digital future of creative Europe—The economic impact of digitization and the Internet on the creative sector in Europe. Booz & Company. Retrieved from http://cercles.diba.cat/documentsdigitals/pdf/E130122.pdf

Le Merle, M., & Le Merle, L. (2015). Capturing the expected returns of angel investors in groups—Less in more, diversify. Fifth Era LLC. Retrieved from https://static1.squarespace.com/static/5481bc79e4b01c4bf3ceed80/t/56a1c90fdc5cb4477ee-852b9/1453443345617/2016+Fifth+Era+-+Less+in+more%2C+-Diversify.pdf

Le Merle, M., & Le Merle, Max. (2016). Do VCs back start-ups? Ensuring start-ups are backed in an innovation cluster. Fifth Era LLC. Retrieved from https://static1.squarespace.com/static/5481bc79e-4b01c4bf3ceed80/t/56d29bf2f699bb6f0be6689c/1456643060069/2016+Fifth+Era+-+Do+VC%27s+back+start-ups%3F.pdf

Le Merle, M., Davis, A., & Le Merle, F. (2016). The Impact of Internet regulation on investment. Fifth Era LLC. Retrieved from https://ennovate.withgoogle.com/uploaded-files/AMIfv94dQN3_ypo-QO23PVxaIcGtjEpAvj6PLGpSCDdGB6V27k8lb-ubTMAHHrX_EClE3U4RRj9Zq73DkYhn8ZIU_Iahm8IQH_aIDFHvh5mZq8Ky-teCBe2IyVoczlo8iCy8FTGAKF_NCitY8dyP4JyNMnXNIU7OcU-1vxtJ4pEpJZYWS00nvNAYEs

Le Merle, M., Le Merle, T., & Engstrom, E. (2014). The impact of Internet regulation on early stage investment. Fifth Era LLC. Retrieved from https://static1.squarespace.com/static/5481bc79e4b01c4bf-3ceed80/t/5487f0d2e4b08e455df8388d/1418195154376/Fifth+Era+report+lr.pdf

Le Merle, M., & Michels, N. (2013). Taking action for tomorrow—California life sciences strategic action plan. Governor of the State of California, Bay Area Council, BayBio, and Monitor Group. Retrieved from http://www.fifthera.com/perspectives-blog/2014/12/9/taking-action-for-tomorrow-bay-area-life-sciences-strategic-action-plan

Le Merle, M., Sarma, R., Ahmed, T., & Pencavel, C. (2011a). The impact of EU Internet copyright regulations on early-stage investment. Booz & Company. Retrieved from http://docs.media.bitpipe.com/io_10x/io_102267/item_485931/Booz&Co%20The%20Impact%20of%20E%20U%20%20Internet%20Copyright%20Regulations%20on%20Early-Stage%20Investment%20A4%2012-15-2011v6.pdf

Le Merle, M., Sarma, R., Ahmed, T., & Pencavel, C. (2011b). The impact of EU Internet privacy regulations on early-stage investment. Booz & Company. Retrieved from http://www.strategyand.pwc.com/

media/uploads/Strategyand-Impact-EU-Internet-Privacy-Regula-tions-Early-Stage-Investment.pdf

Le Merle, M., Sarma, R., Ahmed, T., & Pencavel, C. (2011c). The impact of U.S.Internet copyright regulations on early-stage invest-ment. Booz & Company. Retrieved from http://www.strategyand.pwc.com/media/uploads/Strategyand-Impact-US-Internet-Copy-right-Regulations-Early-Stage-Investment.pdf

Le Merle, M., Sarma, R., Ahmed, T., & Pencavel, C. (2011d). The impact of U.S. Internet privacy regulations on early-stage invest-ment. Booz & Company.

Lerner, J., Schoar, A., Sokolinski, S., & Wilson, K. (2016, February 28). The globalization of angel investments: Evidence across coun-tries. Working paper 16–072. Retrieved from http://www.hbs.edu/faculty/Publication%20Files/16-072_95a38a8a-37e5-4ee2-aa76-9eaee7e5162b.pdf

Maddison, A. (2007). *Contours of the world economy 1–2030 AD: Essays in macro-economic history*. Oxford, U.K.: Oxford University Press.

Marsden, T. C. (2012). Internet co-regulation and constitutionalism: Towards European judicial review. *International Review of Law, Computers & Technology, 26*, 2–3.

Mason, C. M., & Harrison, R. T. (2002). Is it worth it? The rates of returns from informal venture capital investments. *Journal of Busi-ness Venturing, 17*(3), 211–236.

Mason, C. M., & Harrison, R. T. (2011). Annual report on the busi-ness angel market in the United Kingdom: 2009/10. Retrieved from https://www.gov.uk/government/uploads/system/uploads/attach-ment_data/file/32218/11-p116-annual-report-business-angel-mar-ket-uk-2009-10.pdf

May. B., Chen, Jeng-Chung, V., & Wen, K. (2004). The differences of regulatory models and Internet regulation in the European Union and the United States. *Information & Communications Technology Law, 13*(3), 259–272.

May, J., & Liu, M. (Eds.). (2016). *Angels without borders: Trends and policies shaping angel investment worldwide.* Singapore: World Scientific Publishing Company.

McCahery, J., & Vermeulen, E. (2014). Conservatism and innovation in venture capital contracting. *European Business Organization Law Review, 15*(2), 235–266. doi: https://doi.org/10.1017/S1566752914001116

Musyoka, C. (2015). Governments in Africa: Let's support angel investors, key drivers of entrepreneurship. Venture Capital 4 Africa. Retrieved from https://vc4a.com/blog/2015/09/07/governments-in-africa-lets-support-angel-investors-key-drivers-of-entrepreneurship/

National Center for Education Statistics (n.d.). Fast facts: Back to school statistics. Retrieved March 26, 2017, from https://nces.ed.gov/fastfacts/display.asp?id=372

National Venture Capital Association (2013). Venture capital review, Issue 29, Arlington, VA: NVCA. Retrieved from http://www.ey.com/Publication/vwLUAssets/PDF-Venture-Capital-Review-Issue-29_2013/$FILE/Venture-Capital-Review-Issue-29_2013.pdf

National Venture Capital Association (2014). NVCA 2014 yearbook. Arlington, VA: NVCA.

National Venture Capital Association (2015). NVCA 2015 yearbook. Arlington, VA: NVCA.

O'Brien, D. (2008). Copyright challenges for user generated intermediaries: Viacom v YouTube and Google. In B. Fitzgerald, F. Gao, D. O'Brien, & S. Xiaoxiang Shi (Eds.), *Copyright law, digital content and the Internet in the Asia-Pacific* (pp. 219–234). Sydney, Australia: Sydney University Press.

OECD (2011). *Financing high-growth firms: The role of angel investors.* Paris: OECD Publishing.

OECD (2012). *Internet economy outlook 2012.* Paris: OECD Publishing.

OECD (2013). *Entrepreneurship at a glance.* Paris: OECD Publishing.

Pélissié du Rausas, M., Manyika, J., Hazan, E., Bughin, J., Chui, M., & Said, R. (2011, May). Internet matters: The net's sweeping impact on growth, jobs, and prosperity. McKinsey Global Institute. Retrieved from http://www.mckinsey.com/industries/high-tech/our-insights/internet-matters

Perset, K. (2010). The economic and social role of Internet intermediaries. OECD. Retrieved from https://www.oecd.org/internet/ieconomy/44949023.pdf

Porter, M. (1990). *The competitive advantage of nations.* New York, NY: The Free Press.

Porter, M. (1998). Clusters and the new economics of competition. *Harvard Business Review, 76*(6), 77–90.

Porter, M. (2000). Location, competition, and economic development: Local clusters in a global economy. *Journal of Economic Development Quarterly, 14*(1), 241–261.

PricewaterhouseCoopers & National Venture Capital Association (2014). MoneyTree™ report Q1 2014. Retrieved from https://www.pwc.com/us/en/technology/assets/pwc-moneytree-q1-2014-summary-report.pdf

PricewaterhouseCoopers & National Venture Capital Association (2015). MoneyTree™ report Q1 2015. Retrieved from http://www.pwc.com/us/en/technology/assets/pwc-moneytree-q1-2015-summary.pdf

Roach, G. (2010). Is angel investing worth the effort? A study of Keiretsu Forum. *Venture Capital, 12*(2), 153–166. doi: http://dx.doi.

org/10.1080/13691061003643276

Sahlins, M. (1972). "The original affluent society." In *Stone age economics* (1–39). New York, NY: Routledge.

SBA U.S. Small Business Administration (n.d.). Small business facts and infographics. Retrieved March 26, 2017, from https://www.sba.gov/content/small-business-facts-and-infographics

Scheela, W., Isidro, E., Jittrapanun, T., & Trang, N. (2015). Formal and informal venture capital investing in emerging economies in Southeast Asia. *Asia Pacific Journal of Management, 32*(3), 597–617. doi: 10.1007/s10490-015-9420-5

Scheela, W., Isidro, E., Jittrapanun, T., Trang, N., & Gunawan, J. (2012). Business angel investing in emerging economies: Policy implications for Southeast Asia. Paper presented at Kauffman Foundation's International Research and Policy Roundtable, Liverpool, U.K., March 11–12. Retrieved from http://www.kauffman.org/~/media/kauffman_org/z_archive/resource/2012/5/irpr_2012_scheela.pdf

Scientific American (1913). The greatest innovations of our time. *Scientific American CIX*(18).

Smith, Adam. (1776). *The wealth of nations.*

Sohl, J. (2014). The angel investor market in 2014: A market correction in deal size. Center for Venture Research. Durham, NH: University of New Hampshire. Retrieved from https://paulcollege.unh.edu/sites/paulcollege.unh.edu/files/webform/2014%20Analysis%20Report.pdf

Sohl, J. (2015). The angel investor market in 2015: A market correction in deal size. Center for Venture Research. Durham, NH: University of New Hampshire. Retrieved from https://paulcollege.unh.edu/sites/paulcollege.unh.edu/files/webform/Full%20Year%202015%20Analysis%20Report.pdf

Srinivasan, S., Barchas, I., Gorenberg, M., & Simoudis, E. (2014).

Venture capital: Fueling the innovation economy. *Computer, 47*(8), 40–47.

Teare, G., & Desmond, N. (2016). The first comprehensive study on women in venture capital and their impact on female founders. TechCrunch. Retrieved from https://techcrunch.com/2016/04/19/the-first-comprehensive-study-on-women-in-venture-capital/

Umeora, C. (2013). Effects of foreign direct investment (FDI) on economic growth in Nigeria. Available at http://dx.doi.org/10.2139/ssrn.2285329

United Nations (2014). World investment report 2014: Investing in the SDGs: An action plan, Geneva: United Nations, UNCTAD. Retrieved from http://unctad.org/en/PublicationsLibrary/wir2014_en.pdf

United Nations (2015a). World investment report 2015: Reforming international investment governance. Geneva: United Nations, UNCTAD. Retrieved from http://unctad.org/en/PublicationsLibrary/wir2015_overview_en.pdf

United Nations (2015b). World population prospects: The 2015 revision. Geneva: United Nations, Department of Economic and Social Affairs, Population Division. Retrieved from https://esa.un.org/unpd/wpp/publications/files/key_findings_wpp_2015.pdf

Watson, A.M. (1974). The Arab agricultural evolution and its diffusion, 700–1100. *The Journal of Economic History, 34*(1), 8–35.

Weber, R. (2009). Internet of things—Need for a new legal environment? *Computer Law & Security Review, 25*(6), 522–27.

Wiltbank, R. (2009). *Siding with the angels. Business angel investing—Promising outcomes and effective strategies.* U.K.: British Business Angels Association.

Wiltbank, R., & Boeker, W. (2007). Returns to angel investors in groups. Angel Capital Education Foundation. Retrieved from https://

www.angelcapitalassociation.org/data/Documents/Resources/
AngelGroupResarch/1d%20-%20Resources%20-%20Research/
ACEF%20Angel%20Performance%20Project%2004.28.09.pdf

World Economic Forum. (2013, March). The global information technology report, 2013. Geneva: World Economic Forum. Retrieved from https://www.weforum.org/reports/global-information-technology-report-2013

World Economic Forum. (2013, August). The global competitiveness report, 2013–2014. Geneva: World Economic Forum. Retrieved from https://www.weforum.org/reports/global-competitiveness-report-2013-2014

World Economic Forum (2014, April). Delivering digital infrastructure: Advancing the Internet economy. Geneva: World Economic Forum. Retrieved from http://www3.weforum.org/docs/WEF_TC_DeliveringDigitalInfrastructure_InternetEconomy_Report_2014.pdf

Zwillenberg, P., Field, D., & Dean, D. (2014). Connected world series: Greasing the wheels of the Internet economy. The Boston Consulting Group. Retrieved from https://www.icann.org/en/system/files/files/bcg-internet-economy-27jan14-en.pdf

About the Authors

Matthew C. Le Merle

 Matthew Le Merle is co-founder of Fifth Era (www.fifthera.com) and managing partner of Keiretsu Capital, the world's largest angel network and most active US venture investor. For more information go to www.matthewlemerle.com.

Matthew is a sought-after speaker and innovation consultant. He is an expert on digitization and technology transformations having advised leading companies including Bank of America, eBay, EDS, Gap, Genentech, Google, HP, Microsoft, PayPal and Tata/JLR and many other companies on innovation-related issues.

Matthew has advised sovereign and regional economic entities on issues of innovation, entrepreneurialism and cluster growth. Clients have covered the globe from China, the EU, and the UK to the US including in his home state of California and the Bay Area/Silicon Valley.

Matthew's career has spanned being a global strategy advisor, professional services firm leader, corporate operating executive, private equity and venture capital investor, and board director for high growth public and private digital economy companies.

Earlier in his career, Matthew spent 21 years as a strategy consultant and advisor to Fortune 500 CEOs, boards and executive teams with McKinsey & Company, and as a practice leader with EDS/A.T. Kearney and Monitor Group where he led both firms' West Coast practices and at Booz & Company. He was also a corporate executive at Gap Inc. where he was SVP strategy and corporate development and SVP global marketing.

Matthew received a B.A. (Double First) and Master's from Christ Church, Oxford, and an MBA from the Stanford Graduate School of Business. He was born in London, UK, and is now a dual US/UK citizen and lives in the San Francisco Bay Area with his wife, Alison Davis, and their five children.

Alison Davis

Alison Davis is co-founder of Fifth Era (www.fifthera.com). She is a global strategist, finance professional, public company board director and active investor in growth companies. For more information go to www.alisondavis.com.

Alison is currently a director of Royal Bank of Scotland (RBS), Fiserv (FISV), Unisys (UIS) and Ooma (OOMA), and is chair of the advisory board for BlockChain Capital. She is a former director of, City National Bank (CYC), Diamond Foods (DMND), First Data Corporation (FDC), Xoom (XOOM), and many private companies and was the Chairman of LECG (XPRT) until its sale in 2011. She has chaired audit, compensation, and governance committees and is a frequent speaker on corporate governance.

Alison was previously the managing partner of Belvedere Capital, a private equity firm focused on investing in US banks and financial services firms. Prior to this, Alison was the Chief Financial Officer of Barclays Global Investors (now BlackRock), the world's largest institutional investment firm with more than $1.5 trillion of assets under management. Earlier in her career, Alison spent 14 years as a strategy consultant and advisor to Fortune 500 CEOs, boards and executive teams with McKinsey & Company, and as a practice leader with A.T. Kearney where she built and led the global Financial Services Practice.

Alison is active in the community supporting non-profits and social enterprises as a board director, fundraiser and volunteer. She has been frequently named a "Most Influential Women in Business" by the San Francisco Business Times. She received a B.A. Honors and a Master's in Economics from Cambridge University in England, and an MBA from the Stanford Graduate School of Business after completing the first-year at Harvard. She was born in Sheffield, UK, is now a dual US/UK citizen and lives in the San Francisco Bay Area with her husband, Matthew C. Le Merle, and their five children.

About Fifth Era

Fifth Era invests in and incubates early stage technology-enabled companies. The managing team also advises companies and conducts development initiatives to support innovation and growth strategies. For more information go to www.fifthera.com.

MANAGEMENT TEAM

Fifth Era is led by co-founders Matthew C. Le Merle and Alison Davis, globally recognized thought leaders in digital technologies, banking, governance and investment strategies.

INVESTMENT

Fifth Era Capital Fund 1 was formed in 2005 and has invested in 42 companies and exited 11 investments to date.

Fifth Era's managing partner is also managing partner of Keiretsu Capital, the exclusive worldwide fund partner of the world's largest angel network and the most active venture investor in the US.

ADVISORY

Fifth Era works with boards and executive teams of advisory clients to set strategies, identify, conceptualize and launch new businesses, penetrate new markets and drive the corporate growth agenda.

Expertise includes:

- Corporate strategy including facilitation of boards and executive teams
- Mergers and acquisitions, joint ventures, IPOs and fundraising

- Business unit strategy with an emphasis on growth
- Innovation strategy and cultural alignment
- External innovation, collaborative innovation and ecosystem development
- Public and private dialog and business advocacy
- Regulatory policy that stimulates innovation and business formation

PARTNERS

Fifth Era partners with incubators, accelerators and investors as well as worldwide research firms that have the capabilities to provide real-time information and perspective on the issues that concern clients, investors and portfolio companies. The firm maintains an international panel of Internet technology investors and founders.

Acknowledgments

This book draws heavily upon everything we have learned as members of the remarkable San Francisco Bay Area early-stage investment community and all of its participants. For 30 years, we have been around you and you have continuously shared with us new and interesting ideas and insights. We are always surprised by the innovation, optimism, and zeal that greet us every day as we spend our time with you. Thank you.

As angels investors at Keiretsu Forum, Band of Angels, and with the Angel Capital Association of America, we have benefited from the collaborative approach to investing in which we all come together to share our deals, conduct team-based due diligence, and then work together to help our entrepreneurs be successful. We are particularly indebted to our partners at Keiretsu Capital, Randy Williams, who founded Keiretsu Forum 17 years ago, and Nathan McDonald, who is chairman of Keiretsu Forum NorthWest. To these active angel investors we would add additional call-outs: Ian Sobieski and Sonja Markova at Band of Angels and to all the team and angel members of both organizations. At the ACA we would like to explicitly thank Professor Robert Wiltbank, who continues to provide insights into the angel movement through his always-informative research. Other important researchers we have relied upon are detailed in the reference section of this book: we have learned greatly and borrowed significantly from your insights.

Among venture capitalists, we have learned most by watching those general partners whom we have shared boards with: Michael Moritz and Roelof Botha of Sequoia Capital, Dick Kramlich of NEA, and Warren Weiss of Foundation Capital stand out as having been very important in our learning journey. Among stand-alone incubators and accelerators we have found the progress and impact of Rocketspace (Duncan Logan), Runway (Max Shapiro), WeWork (Adam Neuman), and YCombinator (the team) particularly instructive, and the Google Launchpad and Accelerator teams under Roy

Glasberg and the Microsoft BizSpark team under Dan'l Lewin have shown us how to positively impact the lives of hundreds of technology entrepreneurs.

Turning to the technology entrepreneurs themselves, there have been so many along the way that to choose a few might be unfair. Plus, we have learned just as much from the failures in which the aspirations and optimism of the founders turned out to be misplaced as from the successes. However, we would like to make special mention of Alex Fedoseev at 1World Online, Denise Thomas at ApplePie Capital, James Zhang and Jenny Chen at Concept Art House, Linda Jenkinson and Ramesh Patel at LesConcierges, Eric Stang at Ooma, Sunil Saha at Perkville, Brendan O'Driscoll, Aidan Sliney, and Craig Watson at Soundwave (now Spotify), Dan Connors and Kevin Bruner at Telltale Games, and Kevin Hartz at Xoom, as well as the scores of other companies and technology entrepreneurs we have backed - we are sorry we can't name each and every one of you here. We fully appreciate that disruptive innovations begin and end with you and your vision: you are the lead actors in this play.

As to the writing of the book, Matthew C. Le Merle and Alison Davis authored this report, and all errors and omissions are theirs alone. Mark Leonard was our publisher and gave us the confidence to complete the large undertaking of putting our thoughts and perspectives into a book. Nancy Pile was our editor, and Tom Shalvarjian of 3x3 design created the exhibits throughout the book. Sue Balcer created the book interior design, and Katherine Masters designed the covers. Jennifer Bulotti is our press agent and is doing a fantastic job— thank you.

We would like to recognize the significant assistance of our Fifth Era intern team: Miles Honens, Tallulah Le Merle, Maximillian Le Merle, Louis Le Merle, Felix Le Merle, and Leonardo Le Merle, as well as Katie Hamburg and Max Navas at Keiretsu Capital, who provided additional survey results.

Finally, but by no means last, the future is for our children, and this book was written as a guide for them as much as for the thousands of our readers. It took us 30 years and a lot of blind alleys and long diversions to learn what we have tried to synthesize into this book. We give it to you in the hopes that it will save you time and a great deal of energy.

More importantly, we hope that with the insights from this book you can all go out and create a better future—for yourselves, for your friends, and for the world.

Matthew C. Le Merle and Alison Davis
Tiburon, California, USA
April 2017

Disclaimers

Income Disclaimer

This document contains recommendations for business strategies and other business advice that, regardless of our own results and experience, may not produce the same results (or any results) for you. We make absolutely no guarantee, expressed or implied, that by following the advice in this book you will make any money or improve current profits or returns, as there are many factors and variables that come into play regarding any given business or investment strategy.

Primarily, results will depend on the nature of your due diligence, product or business model, the conditions of the marketplace, and situations and elements that are beyond your control.

As with any business endeavor, you assume all risk related to investment and money based on your own discretion and at your own potential expense.

Liability Disclaimer

By reading this document, you assume all risks associated with using the advice given herein, with a full understanding that you, solely, are responsible for anything that may occur as a result of putting this information into action in any way, regardless of your interpretation of the advice.

You further agree that neither we nor our companies can be held responsible in any way for the success or failure of your business or investments as a result of the information presented in this book. It is your responsibility to conduct your own due diligence regarding the safe and successful operation of your business or investment portfolio if you intend to apply any of our information in any way to your business or investment operations.

Terms of Use

You are given a non-transferable "personal use" license to this product. You cannot distribute it or share it with other individuals without the express written permission of the authors.

Also, there are no resale rights or private label rights granted when purchasing this book. In other words, it's for your own personal use only.

Affiliate Relationships Disclosure

We make a number of references in this book to entrepreneurs, companies, or programs that we have invested in, worked with, or recommend. We have no paid affiliate relationship at all with any entrepreneur, company, or program we reference with respect to inclusion in this book.

Stay In Touch with the Authors

Free Updates and Bonus Content!

To receive free book updates, additional content about the topics covered in this book, and find out more about the authors, go to:
BuildYourFortuneInTheFifthEra.com